UK Chamber of Shipping
Understanding UK Shipping

First edition published 2017

ISBN: 978-1-85609-746-8

British Library Cataloguing in Publication Data
A catalogue record for this book is available from the British Library.

Published by

Witherby Publishing Group Ltd
4 Dunlop Square,
Livingston EH54 8SB,
Scotland, UK

+44 (0)1506 463 227
info@witherbys.com
witherbys.com

Printed and bound in Great Britain by Trade Colour Printing, Penrith

Foreword

To an island nation such as the United Kingdom, the importance of shipping is easy to see and difficult to overstate. 95% of our visible international trade is moved by sea.

We depend on shipping to bring finished goods to our shops, whilst the manufacturers of those goods need ships to take raw materials and components to their factories. Lifeline ferries bring isolated communities to the mainland and back, whilst ships carry millions of British holidaymakers to overseas destinations each year.

The United Kingdom shipping industry does much more than move trade and people from one place to the next by sea. It boasts a fleet of advanced ships that support the oil, gas and renewable energy sectors, along with world-leading oceanographic and seismic research vessels, cable-layers and, increasingly, luxury superyachts.

Over 85,000 merchant ships trade internationally, each following rules set at global, regional and national levels. These rules and standards cover almost every area of public policy; from environmental protection to safety, taxation to defence, customs to employment. The United Kingdom has been, and remains, a respected voice at the forefront of the development of the rules under which the industry operates.

This book offers an understanding of those rules for UK shipping; how they are made, how to comply with them and how they affect the industry. It has been written by the UK Chamber of Shipping's team of experts who, as well as having a deep understanding of the regulations, participated in the formulation of many of them. The regulatory framework is continuously evolving and this book considers the regulatory position as it currently stands in spring 2017.

The UK Chamber of Shipping is pleased to present this comprehensive introduction to our vital national industry.

Guy Platten
Chief Executive Officer – UK Chamber of Shipping

Contents

Introduction

1

1.1   Purpose of the Book

This book has been written to provide an introduction to the UK maritime environment and the UK shipping industry. It is a useful introduction to any reader wishing to know more about UK shipping, providing guidance on the legal and administrative processes of shipping in the UK, as well as the numerous regulations that govern ships, ports, crew, trading and operations.

1.2   What do Shipping and the Maritime Sector do?

> Shipping specifically refers to the carriage of goods and persons from one location to another across water. However, in the context of this publication it also includes all vessels that trade upon the seas, for example dredgers, offshore vessels and harbour tugs.

Shipping not only supports world trade, it can positively promote it. Sending goods by sea is by far the most cost effective – and environmentally friendly – means of mass transportation. Comparative studies have found that, per tonne of freight per kilometre carried, ships emit 25 times less CO_2 than aeroplanes, 6 times less than a modern lorry and 3 times less than a modern train.

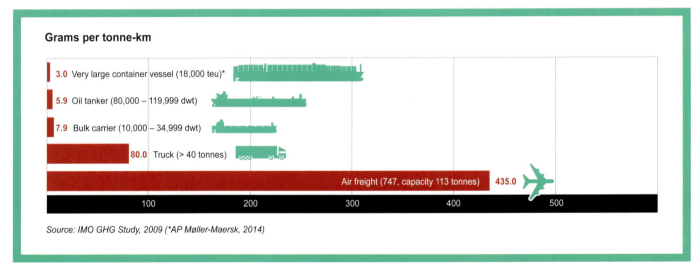

Grams per tonne-km

- **3.0** Very large container vessel (18,000 teu)*
- **5.9** Oil tanker (80,000 – 119,999 dwt)
- **7.9** Bulk carrier (10,000 – 34,999 dwt)
- **80.0** Truck (> 40 tonnes)
- Air freight (747, capacity 113 tonnes) **435.0**

100   200   300   400   500

*Source: IMO GHG Study, 2009 (*AP Møller-Maersk, 2014)*

Figure 1.1: Comparison of typical CO_2 emissions between modes of transport

Ships have evolved to become highly specialised. Tankers are used for the bulk transportation of liquids (crude oils, chemicals, refined products) and gases (liquefied natural gas, liquefied petroleum gas). Bulk carriers for dry cargoes (coal, ores, grain) are categorised broadly into three sizes: Handysize (30,000 deadweight tonnes DWT), Panamax (50,000 – 80,000 DWT) and Capesize (160,000+ DWT). Container ships, which typically carry manufactured or semi-manufactured goods, are measured by the number of 20' containers (TEUs or 20ft equivalent units) they carry. Small container ships (1,000 TEU or less) are used as feeder vessels into smaller ports or rivers, whereas large ocean-going container ships may carry in excess of 20,000 TEU.

There are also cargo ships with refrigerated holds (reefers) that are used to transport fresh produce and a range of specialist vessels designed to carry specific cargoes; for example, livestock carriers, heavy lift vessels and semi-submersibles. There are car carriers, passenger and vehicle carrying vessels, RoRo (Roll-on/Roll-off) ferries, passenger only ferries and cruise ships. In addition, there are specialist function vessels including ice breakers, tugs, offshore support vessels, diving support vessels, accommodation vessels and many different types of drilling rigs. All of these vessels are subject to both international and national regulation and their breadth of design and functions demonstrates the complexity of the shipping industry.

Figure 1.2: Ship types are designed according to their cargo and include bulk carriers, passenger ships, container ships and oil tankers

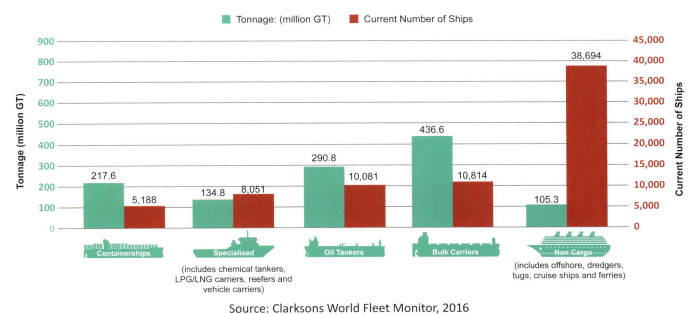

Source: Clarksons World Fleet Monitor, 2016

Figure 1.3: Total ship types and tonnage for the world fleet (2016)

Under UK law, shipping companies are not distinct from any other type of company. Therefore, any UK company that is properly incorporated and constituted may engage in the business of shipping. Supporting these companies is a wide range of ancillary industries and organisations, typically called maritime services. These maritime services ensure that operations and trade are safely and effectively carried out, both domestically and across international boundaries, and include maritime law firms, P&I Clubs, Classification Societies, financial institutions, specialist accounting firms, training organisations, recruitment specialists and many more.

1.3   What is Meant by 'British Shipping'?

The definition of 'British shipping' appears to be simple – British-owned companies operating or owning ships that are registered in the UK and that fly the Red Ensign Flag (the Flag flown by British Merchant Ships). However, the reality is a little more complex. For example, there are several companies that register their vessels either as part of the wider Red Ensign Group (but not in the UK) or in one of the open registries.

The Red Ensign Group (REG) is a group of British Shipping Registers made up from the United Kingdom, the Crown Dependencies (Isle of Man, Guernsey and Jersey) and the UK Overseas Territories (Anguilla, Bermuda, British Virgin Islands, Cayman Islands, Falkland Islands, Gibraltar, Montserrat, St Helena and the Turks & Caicos Islands) that operate shipping registers from their jurisdiction.

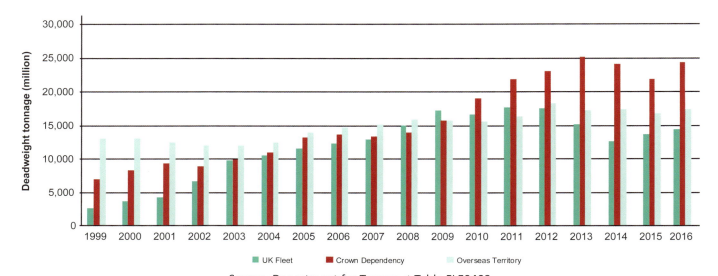

Source: Department for Transport Table FLE0402

Figure 1.4a: Historical tonnage of the Red Ensign Group

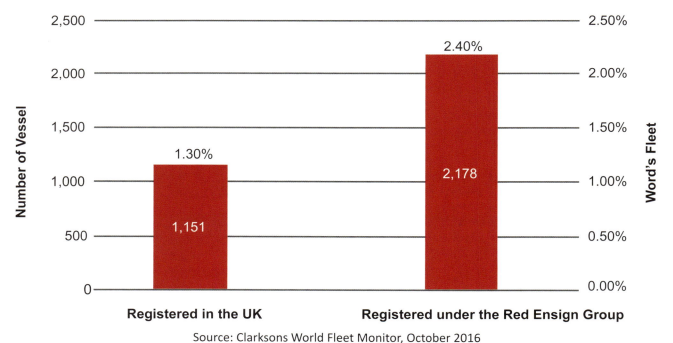

Source: Clarksons World Fleet Monitor, October 2016

Figure 1.4b: Total vessel numbers registered in the UK in 2016

The term 'British Shipping' may also be used to include (in addition to shipowners) ship managers, charterers and those involved in providing maritime services (legal, financial, P&I, Classification Societies etc.).

However, there are certain restrictions to flagging as a number of countries still demand a crew of domestic nationals. For example, vessels eligible for registration in Liberia must be owned by a corporation formed and registered in Liberia. Other countries insist that, for ships to be eligible for registration, a certain percentage of shares in a shipping company must be owned by citizens of that country.

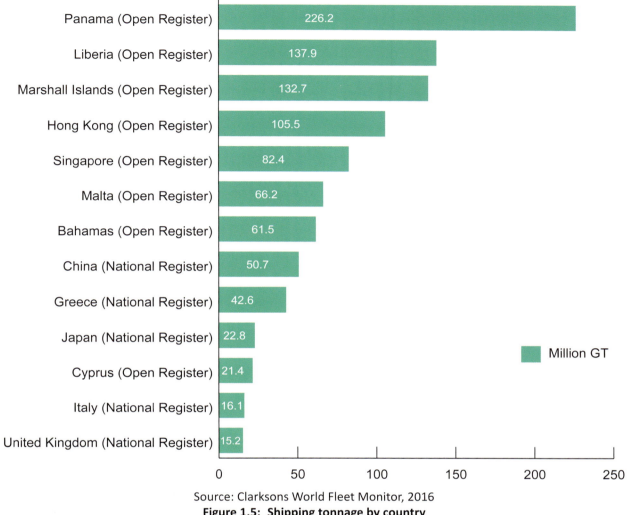

Source: Clarksons World Fleet Monitor, 2016
Figure 1.5: Shipping tonnage by country

Historically, Britain also enforced similar restrictions to flagging and the United Kingdom Merchant Shipping Act 1894 defined a British ship purely in terms of ownership, regardless of whether or not she had been registered in the UK.

This position on ownership was amended, in 1988, to state that for a ship to be British she had to be registered in the UK. This, increasingly, is the view being taken internationally too. However, although this may be the legal view, public perception of what is or is not a British Ship may be different. Passengers using a ferry or taking a cruise with a company that is seemingly quintessentially British would almost certainly consider that they were on a British ship irrespective of the flag flying at the stern of the vessel and the nationality of the crew looking after them.

1.4   Background to British Shipping

1.4.1   Overview

In 2015, the UK shipping industry was estimated to both directly and indirectly contribute to the UK:

- Some 230,000 jobs

- £7.7bn to UK Gross Domestic Product (GDP)

- Over £2bn in tax revenues to the Exchequer

- 95% of all merchandise imports and exports.

However, the merchant fleet has declined dramatically since the start of the 20th century. In 1914, the industry employed a quarter of a million British seafarers, but today this figure is only about 27,000. The number of large British vessels has also dropped, over the last hundred years, from about 3,000 to less than 800.

The reason for this decline is, in part, due to increasing vessel size and the diminishing competitive attractiveness of the UK Flag Administration.

1.4.2   History

Britain made a slow start as a global seafaring nation when compared to other European countries, despite being a major exporter to mainland Europe. It was not until the reign of Elizabeth I in the 16th century that British shipping began to boom, as a direct consequence of the expansion of trade routes in the East and West.

The British trading empire began to take shape during the early 17th century, with the English settlement of North America and the Caribbean and the establishment of joint-stock companies to administer colonies and overseas trade, most notably the East India Company. It has been estimated that by the 18th century one British family in six was directly dependent on the sea for their livelihood.

Britain's trading expansion continued throughout the following century, with overseas commerce carried out within the mercantilist context of the Navigation Acts, (which required that all commodity trade should take place on British ships with British seafarers) and trade between British ports and those within the empire. The repeal of the Navigation Acts in 1849 signalled a change of philosophy to free trade policy.

Figure 1.6: UK-flagged ships from the 18th century to the present day

In wartime, the merchant fleet was essential in keeping the country running, and Britain depended on civilian cargo ships to import food and raw materials, as well as to transport people. By 1939 the British merchant fleet remained the largest in the world, employing some 200,000 men and women, and accounting for around one third of the entire global merchant fleet at the time.

However, things began to decline rapidly in the 1950s when passenger services on ocean routes virtually disappeared and bulk carriers replaced most of the old tramp ships, RoRo vessels revolutionised short sea shipping and road transport took on much of the work of coasters. The increasing transport of gas through undersea pipelines, reduction in the use of coal in power stations and containerisation of most produce and manufactured goods, also all led to a general decline in the number of ships involved in those trades.

From the mid-1950s onwards, the use of standard sized containers to transport goods became the most common method of shipping goods globally. This dramatically reduced transport costs, supporting the post-war boom in international trade, and was a major element in globalisation. Containerisation removed the need for manual sorting and loading of most shipments and displaced many thousands of dock workers and stevedores who had previously handled the cargo. However, containerisation reduced congestion and the time ships spent in ports, significantly shortened shipping time and reduced losses from damage and theft. It proved well suited to transportation by road and rail as well and has since revolutionised intermodal freight transport systems.

The UK government took up 54 merchant ships from trade to be used as troopships and support ships during the Falklands war in 1982. However, despite this large-scale fleet proving effective, the decline of the UK-registered fleet continued. This was partly caused by the growing practice of 'flagging out' to overseas registries in order to remain competitive internationally. In 1975, the size of the UK-owned trading fleet stood at 31.5 million GT and by 1993 this had dwindled to 4.7 million GT.

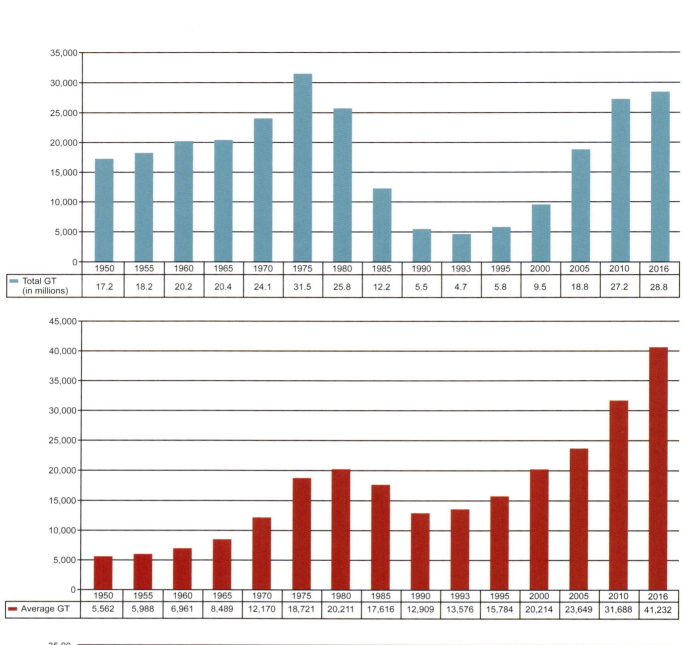

	1950	1955	1960	1965	1970	1975	1980	1985	1990	1993	1995	2000	2005	2010	2016
Total GT (in millions)	17.2	18.2	20.2	20.4	24.1	31.5	25.8	12.2	5.5	4.7	5.8	9.5	18.8	27.2	28.8

	1950	1955	1960	1965	1970	1975	1980	1985	1990	1993	1995	2000	2005	2010	2016
Average GT	5,562	5,988	6,961	8,489	12,170	18,721	20,211	17,616	12,909	13,576	15,784	20,214	23,649	31,688	41,232

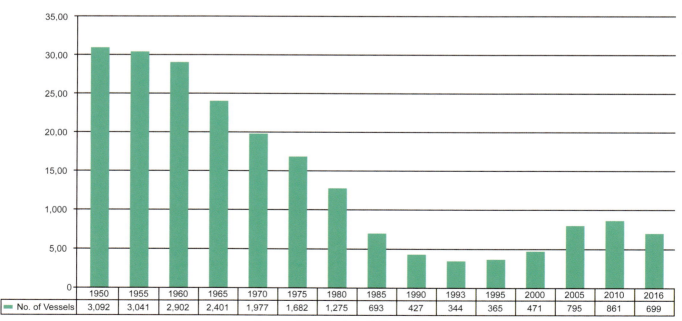

	1950	1955	1960	1965	1970	1975	1980	1985	1990	1993	1995	2000	2005	2010	2016
No. of Vessels	3,092	3,041	2,902	2,401	1,977	1,682	1,275	693	427	344	365	471	795	861	699

Source: DfT Fleet Statistics 2015

Figure 1.7: UK and Crown Dependency (Red Ensign) registered trading vessels, (500 GT and over, 1950–2016)

As can be seen from Figure 1.7, the number of registered trading vessels in the Red Ensign group declined from more than 3,000 in 1950 to a low of 344 in 1993, before experiencing some resurgence and stabilising to 700–800 from 2003 onwards.

While the number of vessels has declined overall, the average size (GT) of vessels has increased significantly, from an average GT of 5,500 in 1950 to more than 39,000 in 2015 – a seven-fold increase.

1.4.3　Tonnage tax

In 2000, the UK Government introduced the Tonnage Tax to try to reverse the decline in fortunes of the UK fleet. Tonnage tax is a method of calculating the taxable profits liable to Corporation Tax of a company whose shipping fleet is 'commercially and strategically managed' in the UK. The tax is determined by applying the ordinary Corporation Tax rate to a fixed notional profit, calculated for the operated ships in the fleet according to their net tonnage. This system is applied in many other countries and is explicitly approved under the EU's state aid policy. The UK regime is unusual in that companies must commit to train new officer trainees every year, in order to nurture and protect UK talent.

Figure 1.8:　A Red Ensign flag and a UK-flagged ferry

1.4.4　Competition

In recent years, competition from other States has intensified and this has encouraged UK ship operators to switch flag, causing a slow decline in the UK-registered fleet. In 2014, the UK Government announced both a review of the Maritime and Coastguard Agency (MCA) and a more far-reaching Maritime Growth Study aimed to further stem decline and promote the UK as a good place from which to conduct maritime business.

A key outcome of the study was the establishment of a Ministerial Working Group for Maritime Growth that will, in collaboration with industry, develop a national strategy for maritime growth. Another was a proposal to reform the MCA and implement procedures for operating the UK Ship Register on a more commercially focused basis. The study also advocated a review of the Government's scheme of Support for Maritime Training (SMarT) and the creation of a single, industry-wide promotional body, working in partnership with Government, to promote and market the UK as a global maritime hub.

1.4.5   Industry bodies

The UK shipping industry is extremely diverse. It includes:

- Shipowners, managers and support services

- Ship builders and marine industries

- Business services including legal, insurance, brokers and financiers

- Ports and port service providers

- Education and training providers.

There are a number of industry bodies that support UK shipping, including:

- The UK Chamber of Shipping, which is the trade association and voice for the UK shipping industry

- A variety of promotional bodies, such as Maritime UK and Maritime London, that provide professional services to the UK shipping industry

- UK Major Ports Group and British Ports Association, which represent the ports industry

- Society of Maritime Industries, which represents the UK's maritime engineering sector

- British Marine, which represents a wide range of companies that are involved in the leisure, super yacht and small commercial marine industry

- Merchant Navy Training Board (MNTB), which sets the training standards for the industry

- Charities for the marine industry, including the Marine Society and Seafarers UK

- Professional organisations for seafarers, including the Nautical Institute, Nautilus and the Honourable Company of Master Mariners.

1.5   Overview of Chapters

Chapter Two – International Regulation

This chapter introduces international regulations, describing how key conventions, notably MARPOL and SOLAS, are developed at the IMO, which is itself supported by a number of other international bodies. The chapter also examines ship registration, Class Societies and the role of the EU in regional regulation.

Chapter Three – Regulation of UK Ships

This chapter looks at how the UK interprets and implements international shipping regulations. Specifically, it examines the various UK regulatory agencies involved in shipping and the processes involved in flagging and certificating in the UK. It also explores some of the considerations an owner will need to assess when making the decision to flag in the UK.

Chapter Four – Crewing and Employment

This chapter familiarises the reader with the most important considerations that a ship operator will have with regard to crewing their ships, covering laws dealing with crew nationality, training and qualifications and the provision of decent living and working conditions. Furthermore, it examines UK employment laws, the special arrangements for income tax and National Insurance contributions that apply to employment on board ship and standards of occupational health and safety.

Chapter Five – Running a Shipping Business in the UK

This chapter outlines the regulatory and fiscal framework for establishing and running a shipping business in the UK. It outlines the special provisions for companies that own and operate ships and covers other regulatory requirements (such as those relating to visas for overseas personnel, to business ethics and to sanctions) that impact shipping companies due to the global nature of their business.

Chapter Six – The UK Shipping Market

The UK has an open coast policy, with no restrictions on the ships that may carry goods to or from a UK port or on the shipowners who can compete for business from UK customers. This chapter sets out the statutory underpinning for this policy and shows its significance by comparing it with the position in other countries.

Chapter Seven – Trading and Operating a Ship

This chapter explains the shoreside aspects of operating and managing a ship. It makes particular reference to the International Safety Management (ISM) Code and the maritime security requirements contained in the International Ship and Port Facility Security (ISPS) Code, which apply to both ships and shoreside facilities. It also includes a brief description of Bills of Lading (B/Ls) and the Carriage of Goods by Sea.

Chapter Eight – Ports and their Customers

This chapter explains the management of the UK's harbour organisations, the means of ensuring navigational and other safe operations, including pilotage. It also explains the aids to navigation that exist in UK waters.

Chapter Nine – Customs Rules

This chapter outlines the customs controls that apply to maritime trade. It examines the obligations of shipping companies as carriers of goods, and how these differ depending on whether a ship's voyage is domestic or international. The chapter also outlines the customs rules that apply to ships' stores and equipment.

Chapter Ten – Passenger Shipping

This chapter outlines the regulatory regime that applies to the carriage of passengers, examining how consumer rights, rules and laws designed to regulate individuals' behaviour apply on ships. It also summarises the complex array of border controls that apply to passengers arriving in the UK by ferry or cruise ship.

International Regulation

2.1   Introduction

Figure 2.1: IMO Headquarters, London

This chapter introduces the international nature of regulation and describes how the maritime regulatory environment has developed and now operates across the globe. Relevant international agencies are described and some of the key conventions and codes are discussed.

The freedom to navigate unhindered on the high seas is a fundamental right that allows access for all vessels, irrespective of nationality, to all waters that are not the internal waters of a State. This is set out in the United Nations Convention on the Law of the Sea (UNCLOS), which was adopted in 1982 and came into force in 1994. It replaced earlier treaties and the historical concept of 'freedom of the seas', which dated back to the 17th century. Key features of the treaty are navigational rights, territorial sea limits, economic jurisdiction, the passage of ships through narrow straits, and protection and management of the marine environment and its resources. It gives coastal States sovereignty over their territorial waters and limits the rights of foreign vessels in territorial waters belonging to another State.

International law also lays down a framework of rules for shipping and looks to individual States to enforce and ensure compliance with these rules through jurisdiction exercised over their national vessels. The nationality of a vessel conveys both compliance with and protection by the laws of that State. The decision on where to register and flag a vessel is, therefore, of huge importance, both administratively and commercially.

2.2   How and why the Shipping Industry is Regulated

Ships operate and trade internationally, making shipping an inherently global industry, but it would be problematic both commercially and administratively if ships from different States visiting the same port were subject to completely different regulatory regimes. For the port being visited, the host authorities would also find it unacceptable to have vessels with completely different standards of safety in their waters. A lower standard would present a higher risk of pollution or a casualty occurring, so internationally agreed regulations and enforceable standards are both necessary and desirable.

The regulation of shipping has existed for centuries. It is thought that legislation existed to control the safe loading and maintenance of the earliest vessels and laws governing the life and working conditions on board ships are known to have been in place as early as the 14th century. Often, this historic legislation was a response to a specific event – the enquiry following the loss of the RMS 'Titanic' in 1912 recommended that an international conference be convened, the outcome of which was the International Convention for the Safety of Life at Sea (SOLAS) 1914, the first international maritime convention.

Figure 2.2: RMS 'Titanic'

More recently, concern about pollution and the impact of shipping on the environment has led to the establishment of the International Convention for the Prevention of Pollution from Ships (MARPOL).

Figure 2.3: Regulations exist to prevent the occurrence of oil spills such as this

The body responsible for SOLAS and MARPOL is the International Maritime Organization (IMO), a specialised agency of the United Nations. While SOLAS and MARPOL are the main conventions concerned with the safety of life and protection of the environment, there are now many other codes and conventions derived from them, providing a framework for ship design and construction, safety equipment to be carried on board, how the vessel is operated, maintained and manned, as well as the training of seafarers. Once ratified, these instruments and the amendments to them are adopted into national legislation by contracting governments.

The conventions largely govern ships on international voyages. The safety of domestic vessels, providing domestic services, and rules that take account of local conditions and trading patterns, are predominantly the responsibility of individual States or, in some cases, regional authorities. However, in some areas, such as the safety of navigation, international conventions must be followed. Ship operators and Masters need to observe international, regional and national regulations. The competence and rights of seafarers are also strictly controlled through regulations such as the International Convention on Standards of Training, Certification and Watchkeeping for Seafarers (STCW) and the Maritime Labour Convention (MLC); the latter addresses the welfare of seafarers and is produced by the International Labour Organization (ILO) (see Chapter 4 for further details of STCW and the MLC).

2.3   The Global Bodies

Maritime Treaties, Codes, Conventions and Guidelines originate from international regulatory sources, such as the International Maritime Organization (IMO) and the International Labour Organization (ILO).

Applicable international legislation is then implemented by the UK Government, either through an Act of Parliament (such as the Merchant Shipping Act) or via secondary legislation (in the form of Statutory Instruments, under powers assigned to the Department for Transport).

Maritime & Coastguard Agency

Regulations and Guidance are then coordinated through the Maritime and Coastguard Agency (MCA), the specific executive agency for all maritime matters in the UK.

The MCA issues Marine (M) Notices to companies, ships, merchant navy officers and shore organisations. These take the form of:

- Merchant Shipping Notices (MSNs)
- Marine Guidance Notes (MGNs)
- Marine Information Notes (MINs).

2.3.1 The International Maritime Organization (IMO)

Figure 2.4: The main hall assembly chamber of the IMO

The IMO is an agency of the United Nations and, with its Member States, it is responsible for the regulation of shipping. It was established in 1948 as a permanent international body capable of developing and adopting legislation related to maritime safety, and has its headquarters in London. The first Assembly met in January 1959, with 28 Member States from the traditional maritime nations of the northern hemisphere, and focused primarily on the update and amendment of SOLAS. It now has 171 Member States and a number of non-governmental organisations have observer status. Its remit has expanded beyond the safety of life at sea to include environmental concerns, legal issues, technical cooperation, maritime security and seafarer training.

The governing body is the Assembly of members, which meets every two years. A Council, consisting of 40 Member States elected by the Assembly, meets more regularly. There is a secretariat of 300 international civil servants headed by an elected Secretary General. Technical business is conducted by the five committees and a number of sub-committees:

List of IMO committees and sub-committees

IMO Committees:
- Maritime Safety Committee (MSC)
- Marine Environment Protection Committee (MEPC)
- Legal Committee
- Technical Cooperation Committee (for capacity building)
- Facilitation Committee (to simplify the documentation and formalities required in international shipping).

MSC and MEPC Sub-Committees:
- Human Element, Training and Watchkeeping (HTW)
- Implementation of IMO instruments (III)
- Navigation, Communications and Search and Rescue (NCSR)
- Pollution Prevention and Response (PPR)
- Ship Design and Construction (SDC)
- Ship Systems and Equipment (SSE)
- Carriage of Cargoes and Containers (CCC).

Work in the committees and sub-committees, and in some cases working groups and correspondence groups, is undertaken by representatives of the Member States, with other governmental and non-governmental organisations (NGOs) providing their input. The bulk of work is concerned with the amendment of existing conventions; proposals for new conventions must be approved by the Assembly or Council and are adopted following an international conference.

Entry into force occurs when the requisite criteria has been met, which may be ratification by a certain number of signatories, with a certain minimum combined tonnage. Once entered into force, signatories are obliged to fulfil the requirements of the regulations and adopt them into domestic legislation as appropriate.

The IMO has no powers of enforcement and it is for contracting governments to carry out this function, usually by the survey and inspection of ships on their own register and those visiting ports within their territory.

2.3.2   The International Hydrographic Organization (IHO)

The IHO is an intergovernmental organisation established in 1921 to support the safety of navigation and the protection of the marine environment. Its main functions are to ensure the supply of nautical charts and hydrographic services across the world and to achieve uniformity in nautical charts and documents. The IHO is also responsible for coordinating the activities of national hydrographic offices; for the UK, this is the United Kingdom Hydrographic Office (UKHO).

Figure 2.5: Charts are produced for navigation by national hydrographic authorities, who are coordinated through the IHO

2.3.3   The International Association of Classification Societies (IACS)

IACS is a non-governmental organisation comprised of the 12 leading Classification Societies, with a secretariat based in London. The International Load Line Convention of 1930 recommended that Classification Societies should collaborate to achieve "*as much uniformity as possible in the application of the standards of strength upon which freeboard is based …*". The Registro Italiano Navale (RINA) subsequently hosted the first conference of the leading Societies in 1939, attended by the American Bureau of Shipping (ABS), Bureau Veritas (BV), DNV GL, Lloyd's Register (LR) and Nippon Kaiji Kyokai (Class NK), and IACS was formed.

The value of their combined technical knowledge and experience is such that IACS has consultative status at the IMO. They provide technical support, guidance and unified interpretations of the international statutory regulations. These interpretations are applied by each IACS member society when certifying compliance with the statutory regulations on behalf of authorising Flag States.

Figure 2.6: Maritime Classification Societies exist to help ensure ships are constructed safely and to required international standards

2.4 Safety of Life and Protection of the Environment

2.4.1 International Convention for the Safety of Life at Sea (SOLAS)

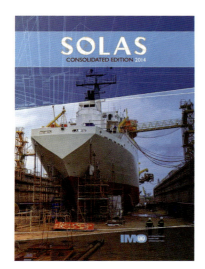

Figure 2.7: SOLAS

SOLAS ensures that ships comply with minimum safety standards relating to construction, equipment and operation.

The origins of the Convention follow the loss of the RMS *'Titanic'*, which struck an iceberg in April 1912. Of the 2,224 people on board, more than 1,500 perished. The subsequent enquiry by Lord Mersey, the UK's Wreck Commissioner, produced the following final recommendation:

24. That (unless already done) steps should be taken to call an International Conference to consider and as far as possible to agree upon a common line of conduct in respect of (a) the subdivision of ships; (b) the provision and working of life-saving appliances; (c) the installation of wireless telegraphy and the method of working the same; (d) the reduction of speed or the alteration of course in the vicinity of ice; and (e) the use of searchlights.

The UK Government proposed a conference to develop international regulations, which took place in London and was attended by representatives of 13 countries. The subsequent treaty was adopted on 20th January 1914 and consisted of the following requirements:

The Requirements Stemming from SOLAS

1. Safe navigation for all merchant ships

2. The provision of watertight and fire-resistant bulkheads

3. Life-saving appliances

4. Fire prevention and fire-fighting appliances on passenger ships

5. Carriage of radiotelegraph equipment for ships carrying more than 50 persons

6. Establishment of a North Atlantic ice patrol.

The Convention entered into force in July 1915 and four subsequent versions have since been developed. In 1929, navigation aids and rules to prevent collisions were added. Other versions were negotiated in 1948 and 1960 in response to advancing technology. Then, mindful of the time required to renegotiate the Convention, it was decided instead to adopt the Tacit Acceptance procedure to ensure that changes could be made within a specified (and acceptably short) period of time. Instead of requiring acceptance by a specified proportion of Parties, amendments would enter into force on a specified date unless objections were received from an agreed number of Parties. The current version of SOLAS was adopted in 1974 at a conference attended by 71 countries. It now lays down a comprehensive range of minimum standards for the safe construction of ships (stability, the number of subdivisions within a ship, watertight integrity etc.) and the basic safety equipment (fire protection, navigation, life-saving and radio) to be carried on board. It also requires regular ship surveys and the issue by Flag States of certificates of compliance.

Chapter Headings of SOLAS

Chapter I	General Provisions
Chapter II-1	Construction: subdivision and stability, machinery and electrical installations
Chapter II-2	Fire protection, fire detection and fire extinction
Chapter III	Life-saving appliances and arrangements
Chapter IV	Radiocommunications
Chapter V	Safety of navigation
Chapter VI	Carriage of cargoes
Chapter VII	Carriage of dangerous goods
Chapter VIII	Nuclear ships
Chapter IX	Management for the safe operation of ships
Chapter X	Safety measures for high-speed craft
Chapter XI-1	Special measures to enhance maritime security
Chapter XI-2	Special measures to enhance maritime security
Chapter XII	Additional safety measures for bulk carriers
Chapter XIII	Verification of compliance
Chapter XIV	Safety measures for ships operating in polar waters

Applicability of SOLAS is laid down in Chapter I, Regulation 1, which states that:

'Unless expressly provided otherwise, the present regulations apply only to ships engaged on international voyages.'

Regulation 3 gives exceptions:

a. *The present regulations, unless expressly provided otherwise, do not apply to:*

   i. *Ships of war and troopships*

   ii. *Cargo ships of less than 500 GT*

   iii. *Ships not propelled by mechanical means*

   iv. *Wooden ships of primitive build*

   v. *Pleasure yachts not engaged in trade*

   vi. *Fishing vessels.*

As does Chapter V – Safety of Navigation, where Regulation 1 states that:

'Unless expressly provided otherwise, this chapter shall apply to all ships on all voyages, except: … those on Government non-commercial service …'

SOLAS remains the cornerstone of safety at sea and continues to evolve under the direction of the IMO. The mandatory carriage of an Electronic Chart Display Information System (ECDIS) for certain ship types, to improve navigational safety, and the introduction of the Polar Code, for vessels operating in the Arctic and Antarctic regions, are among the most recent amendments.

Figure 2.8: The most recent chapter to SOLAS is Chapter XIV on the Polar Code

2.4.2   International Convention for the Prevention of Pollution from Ships (MARPOL)

As well as the safety of life at sea, protection of the marine environment has been of concern to national governments since at least the early 1920s, when local regulations to control discharges of oil in their territorial waters were introduced. In 1954, the United Kingdom organised the first conference related to sea pollution 'International Convention for the Prevention of Pollution of the Sea by Oil'. The functions and the regulations of the Convention were later passed to the IMO. A spate of tanker accidents, notably the *'Torrey Canyon'* in 1967, galvanised the international community and the International Convention for the Prevention of Pollution from Ships 1973 (MARPOL) followed. However, as its entry into force was delayed, the Convention was absorbed by the 1978 MARPOL Protocol. The new combined treaty entered into force on 2nd October 1983. In 1997, a new Annex was added, which entered into force on 19th May 2005.

MARPOL has been continuously updated by amendments to reflect policy and technical developments and it is the main international convention addressing pollution from ships. Its provisions aim to prevent and control pollution of the marine environment and maritime accidents. It prohibits the discharge of any type of substance harmful to the marine environment and it has contributed to the significant decrease in pollution from international shipping over the past decades, as well as greatly improving ship construction and navigation standards.

Figure 2.9: MARPOL exists to ensure that pollution is prevented in the marine environment

The Convention currently includes six technical Annexes. They include requirements and standards for certificates and record books as well as requirements for Port States to provide adequate reception facilities for waste and cargo residues.

Annex I – Regulations for the Prevention of Pollution by Oil

This covers prevention of pollution by oil from operational measures as well as from accidental discharges. It sets out special sea areas where tighter restrictions apply, design criteria for oil tankers, oily water discharge limits, the requirement to carry an oil record book and emergency oil pollution plans. Amendments in 1992 made it mandatory for new oil tankers to have double hulls as a result of the *'Exxon Valdez'* incident.

Annex II – Regulations for the Control of Pollution by Noxious Liquid Substances in Bulk

MARPOL requires chemical carriers to comply with the International Code for the Construction and Equipment of Ships carrying Dangerous Chemicals in Bulk (IBC Code). The Code includes design and construction standards for ships and the equipment that they should carry, with due regard to the polluting impact of the products involved. Noxious liquid substances in bulk are divided into four categories related to their properties as potential marine pollutants (X, Y, Z and other substances, which are not harmful to the marine environment and therefore Annex II does not apply).

Subsequently, three types of chemical carriers have been designed to meet the carriage requirements of these products. Type 1 is designed for the transportation of products that present the greatest hazard and types 2 and 3 for products of progressively lesser hazard. Every chemical tanker is required to carry a Certificate of Fitness that lists the products it is permitted to carry as well as a Procedures and Arrangements (P&A) Manual that provides marine environment aspects of cleaning of cargo tanks and the discharge of cargo residues.

Annex III – Prevention of Pollution by Harmful Substances Carried by Sea in Packaged Form

Unlike Annexes I and II, Annex III is optional and Governments ratifying MARPOL may choose not to accept its provisions. Annex III applies to all ships involved in the carriage of harmful substances in packaged form, e.g. container vessels, ferries etc. It contains general requirements for the issuing of detailed standards on packing, marking, labelling, documentation, stowage, quantity limitations, exceptions and notifications for preventing pollution by harmful substances. According to Annex III, harmful substances are those identified as marine pollutants in the IMDG Code.

Annex IV – Prevention of Pollution by Sewage from Ships

This contains requirements for setting discharge limits for treated and untreated sewage. It requires ships to be equipped with either an approved sewage treatment plant, an approved sewage comminuting and disinfecting system or a sewage holding tank. Comminuted and disinfected sewage can be discharged more than three nautical miles from the nearest land, otherwise untreated sewage can be discharged more than 12 nautical miles from the nearest land. In any case, sewage shall not be discharged instantaneously but at a moderate rate when the ship is en route and proceeding at more than four knots.

Annex V – Prevention of Pollution by Garbage from Ships

This Annex sets requirements regarding the disposal of garbage from ships. It prohibits the disposal of all types of garbage, with the exception of food waste, animal carcasses and non-marine-pollutant cargo residues. Annex V imposes a complete ban on the disposal into the sea of all forms of plastic and requires that shipboard-generated garbage be segregated into nine categories (plastic, food waste, cargo residues, etc.). Ships are required to carry a Garbage Management Plan and maintain a Garbage Record Book. Eight special areas have been established under the Annex, where special discharge requirements apply.

Annex VI – Prevention of Air Pollution from Ships

Annex VI sets limits on sulphur oxide (SOx) and nitrogen oxide (NOx) emissions from ship exhausts and prohibits deliberate emissions of ozone-depleting substances; designated emission control areas (ECAs) set more stringent standards for SOx, NOx and particulate matter. These have been established in the North Sea, Channel and Baltic and around the coast of North America, with several more ECAs planned worldwide.

The seas around North America have also been designated as a NOx ECA. A chapter adopted in 2011 covers mandatory technical and operational energy efficiency measures aimed at reducing greenhouse gas emissions from ships. For new ships, this meant the introduction of the Energy Efficiency Design Index (EEDI), which is specific for each ship type and promotes the use of more energy-efficient machinery and propulsion systems.

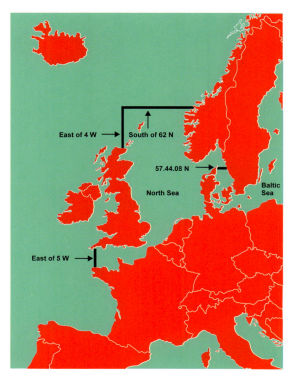

Figure 2.10: The Sulphur ECA around the UK and the North Sea

At MEPC 70, in October 2016, the IMO designated the North Sea and the Baltic Sea as a NOx ECA from 1ˢᵗ January 2021 onwards. This NECA applies to all vessels built after 2021 and requires NOx emissions to be reduced by 80% compared to the present emission level.

2.4.3   International Convention on Load Lines (CLL), 1966

The Load line Convention sets the maximum levels to which a ship can be loaded so that safe freeboard is maintained under varying conditions of water density and seasonal considerations (see Figure 2.11 for details of the world zones).

By the mid-19ᵗʰ century, the overloading of cargo ships had become a major problem. Many ships were being lost as a result and there were calls for regulation, led by Samuel Plimsoll, a member of the UK Parliament. Legislation was finally introduced and by 1870 the British government required vessels bear a load line, marked on the hull at the waterline. This would indicate whether the vessel was overloaded and so ensure the safety of crew and cargo.

The first International Convention on Load Lines was adopted in 1930 and was based on the reserve buoyancy of the vessel. This was further developed and led to the International Convention on Load Lines (CLL), 1966. The Convention included provisions for determining freeboard, the number of watertight compartments and damage stability calculations. It was amended by the 1988 Protocol and further revised in 2003. The basic requirement was for ships engaged in international voyages to have assigned load lines marked amidships on each side. The required freeboard and position of the lines are verified by Classification Societies, who issue an International Load Line Certificate for the ship.

2.4.4   Convention on the International Regulations for Preventing Collisions at Sea (COLREGs), 1972

The COLREGs lay down the rules of the road for ships, i.e. the requirement for visual, light and sound signals, the requirement to keep a good lookout and rules for traffic separation schemes (TSS).

The current regulations evolved from the many separate rules practised in different parts of the world. For the UK, the Steam Navigation Act 1846 included regulations drawn up by Trinity House. These were updated in 1863 and subsequently adopted by many other States. The rules were subsequently developed through an international conference in 1889 and during the SOLAS conferences at the IMO. The current rules were adopted by the IMO on 20ᵗʰ October 1972 and entered into force on 15ᵗʰ July 1977.

The rules apply to all vessels on the high seas and are brought into effect in territorial waters through national legislation. Fundamental to their understanding is that vessels are either obliged to give way or stand on. There is no right of way as such, indeed in a head-on situation both vessels are required to give way and, in some circumstances, it may well be necessary for a stand-on vessel to take the avoiding action.

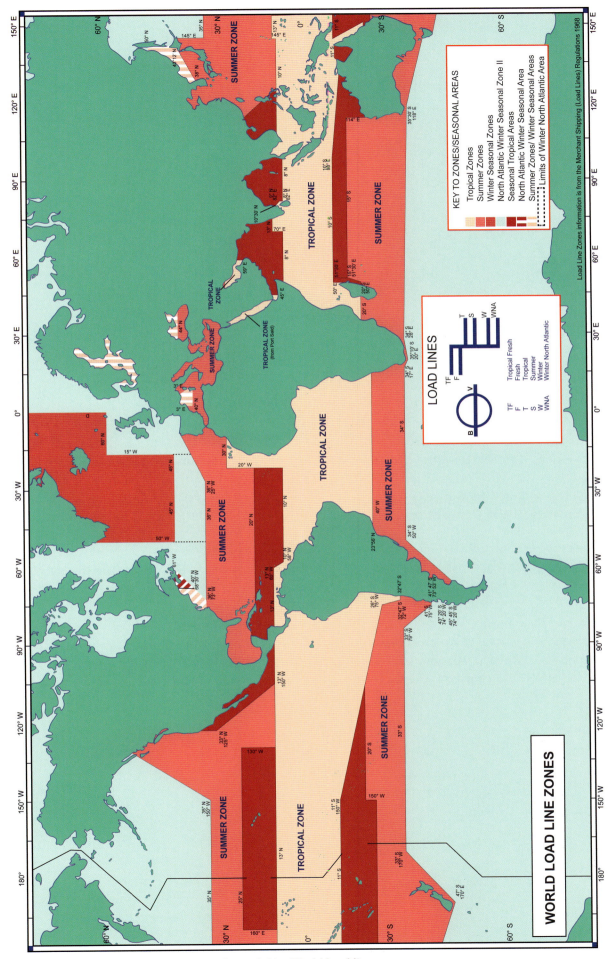

Figure 2.11: World load line zones

Figure 2.12: COLREGs prevent collisions at sea by establishing clear rules for collision avoidance

2.4.5   International Convention for the Control and Management of Ships' Ballast Water and Sediments (BWM Convention)

Ballast water is used on ships to help manage and control the stability of the vessel during unloading and loading operations. For example, an oil tanker discharging its cargo to a port will have to correspondingly fill up its ballast water tanks in order to increase the stability of the ship.

The Ballast Water Management (BWM) Convention (2004) sets out standards to prevent marine pollution by controlling the discharge of ships' ballast water. This prevents invasive species from ballast water taken from one environment damaging a different marine environment as they are discharged. The Convention took many years to pass, but eventually did so in 2016 for entry into force in 2017. Compliance with the Convention is of both a technical and operational nature.

Figure 2.13: A ship discharging ballast water

2.4.6   Cargo safety

The stability of a vessel can be affected by its cargo. Cargoes can also be inherently dangerous, while others may become dangerous if they get wet or are not properly ventilated. Dangerous and explosive gases can build up and cargoes can 'liquefy', which can have a detrimental effect on ship stability. In the worst cases, this can lead to fire, explosion or capsize and loss of the vessel. Rules and standards for cargoes are set by SOLAS and MARPOL, which in turn inform a number of other mandatory and non-mandatory Codes.

Figure 2.14:   Loading and unloading a ship is dangerous if not done correctly and in accordance with procedures

International Maritime Solid Bulk Cargoes (IMSBC) Code

The IMSBC Code is mandatory and aims to ensure the safety of solid bulk cargoes by providing information on the dangers associated with the shipment of such cargoes. This includes an awareness of the properties of materials and potential risks in their shipment, together with any procedures to be followed, such as testing for moisture content prior to embarkation. High moisture content and subsequent liquefaction during passage may cause the cargo to shift, leading to instability of the ship and possible capsize.

Figure 2.15: A bulk carrier

The Code groups cargoes as:

- Group A – cargoes that may liquefy

- Group B – cargoes that possess a chemical hazard

- Group C – neither Group A nor Group B, but could still be hazardous.

These groups are used to describe each cargo's properties and detail the requirements for handling, stowing and safe carriage. Carrying solid bulk cargoes involves serious risks that must be managed carefully to safeguard the crew and the ship.

International Maritime Dangerous Goods (IMDG) Code

The IMDG Code was developed for dangerous goods being shipped in packaged form. It sets out requirements for various substances, materials or articles and covers matters such as packing, stowage and segregation from other, incompatible, substances. It became mandatory in 2004, although some parts remain recommendatory.

International Convention for Safe Containers (CSC)

The rapid increase in the use of freight containers for the transport of goods by sea, and the subsequent development of specialised container ships, saw the need to assure the safety of this type of cargo. The Convention for Safe Containers has two goals: first, to provide test procedures and related strength requirements and, second, to provide uniform international safety regulations that are equally applicable to all modes of surface transport.

International Code for the Construction and Equipment of Ships carrying Dangerous Chemicals in Bulk (IBC) Code

The IBC Code provides an international standard for the safe bulk carriage by sea of dangerous chemicals and noxious liquid substances. It prescribes the design and construction standards of ships and specifies equipment to be carried.

Code of Safe Practice for Cargo Stowage and Securing (CSS Code)

The CSS Code was adopted in 1991 and is regularly reviewed and amended. It provides an international standard for the safe stowage and securing of cargoes in order to prevent ship casualties, injuries and loss of life. It includes the general principles of stowage and securing as well as requirements for planning and executing cargo operations and information for personnel to carry out tasks safely.

International Code for the Safe Carriage of Grain in Bulk (Grain Code)

The Grain Code was adopted in 1991 to help ensure the safe carriage of grain cargoes in bulk. Grain has a tendency to shift and settle, creating stability issues for the vessel. The Code identifies the nature of grain cargoes, such as wheat, oats or barley, and sets out standards for safe cargo operations.

International Code for the Construction and Equipment of Ships Carrying Liquefied Gases in Bulk (IGC Code)

The IGC Code, adopted in 1983 and revised extensively since then, contains the requirements for liquefied gas ships, taking into account recent technical developments in the gas maritime sector. The Code covers ship design, safety arrangements, cargo containment, loading, discharging and fire/accident controls.

In addition to the Codes and Conventions stated here, an outline of the ISM and ISPS Codes is contained in Chapter 7 – Trading and Operating a Ship and an outline of the MLC Convention is contained in Chapter 4 – Crewing and Employment.

2.5   Enforcement and the Concept of Nationality

To be effective, any regulatory activity must be supported by a means of enforcement. When international conventions are ratified by national governments, the various articles of the convention are incorporated into domestic law. That government is then obliged to enforce the articles of the convention.

2.5.1   Ship registration

To demonstrate compliance with the law, all ships must be registered with a State that has a ship registry. This country then becomes the vessel's Flag State. A ship operator may choose which Flag State to register a vessel with and the choice can be one of the most important decisions owners make. Ship registration has existed for centuries and Member States of the EU have kept national registers since the 17th century. Today, the right to establish and maintain a register of its ships is recognised as the sovereign right of every State.

The act of registration varies from State to State, but entitles a ship to fly the flag of the State concerned as a symbol of belonging to it. In turn, by accepting a ship onto its register, the Flag State acquires sovereign rights over it and assumes various duties in relation to it.

Figure 2.16: A container ship registered in London

Historically, shipowners were required to register their ship in their State of residence (or in the State in which they carried out their business). Modern ship registration is much more diverse:

- **National Registry:** A registry that is only open to ships owned by its own nationals or incorporated companies

- **Open Registry:** A registry that is open to foreign-owned ships

- **International Registry:** These offer the pride and protection of a national flag, but may be more commercially competitive, permitting, for example, the hiring of foreign seafarers for crew. Countries such as Norway, Denmark and the Isle of Man are international registries.

2.5.2   The practical consequences of ship registration

Registering a ship with a particular Flag State brings it within the law of that State; Flag States must enforce legislation on board vessels. Registration identifies the jurisdiction under which a ship operates and its regulatory regime, including construction standards, details of equipment carried, documentation and manning. It gives ships the right to navigate freely in international waters, make innocent passage through territorial waters and access foreign ports – all the major components in a ship's ability to trade.

The process of adopting international conventions, some of which may be unintentionally ambiguous or lack detail, into domestic law leads to variations in interpretation between different States and some States may interpret the conventions more rigorously than others.

As well as international maritime safety standards, many Flag States also enforce national laws on board ships on their registers (for example smoking bans or legislation covering crews' pay). As national laws often vary between States, this results in discrepancies in compliance costs for ships on different registers.

Inspections are carried out by Flag States, or agents employed to act on their behalf, to ensure compliance with these international and national standards and certificates are issued to ships as supporting evidence.

2.5.3   Port State Control (PSC)

Enforcement of international regulation within the territory, for example when a foreign ship is visiting a port of that territory, is known as Port State Control (PSC). This is achieved through inspection and examination of documentary evidence to confirm compliance. This responsibility is undertaken by a specified maritime department or agency of the host country.

Figure 2.17: Port State Control inspections ensure that ships are compliant and safe

In 1982, several European countries agreed upon the Paris Memorandum of Understanding (MoU), which established a supplementary regime of Port State Control in response to the fluctuating performance of several Flag States in enforcing international standards. The Paris MoU stipulated that ships registered under flags with a poor record of ensuring compliance would be inspected more frequently than others when visiting European ports. The Paris MoU is just one of several regional arrangements for Port State Control that exist globally (for example, the Tokyo MoU was agreed in 1993) and the results of these regional inspections are compiled in annual league tables. These league tables are known as white, grey or black lists, and the ranking of a particular flag will depend on the performance at inspection of ships flying that flag. Historically, national registers upheld the strongest regulatory oversight and standards, but many open registers are now among the most highly respected.

Coordinated inspections are often carried out regionally, with emphasis placed on ships registered under less reputable flags or those with a known history of sub-standard safety records.

> The regions operate under various memorandums of understanding:
>
> - Europe and the North Atlantic (Paris MoU)
> - Asia and the Pacific (Tokyo MoU)
> - Latin America (Acuerdo de Viña del Mar)
> - Caribbean (Caribbean MoU)
> - West and Central Africa (Abuja MoU)
> - Black Sea region (Black Sea MoU)
> - Mediterranean (Mediterranean MoU)
> - Indian Ocean (Indian Ocean MoU).

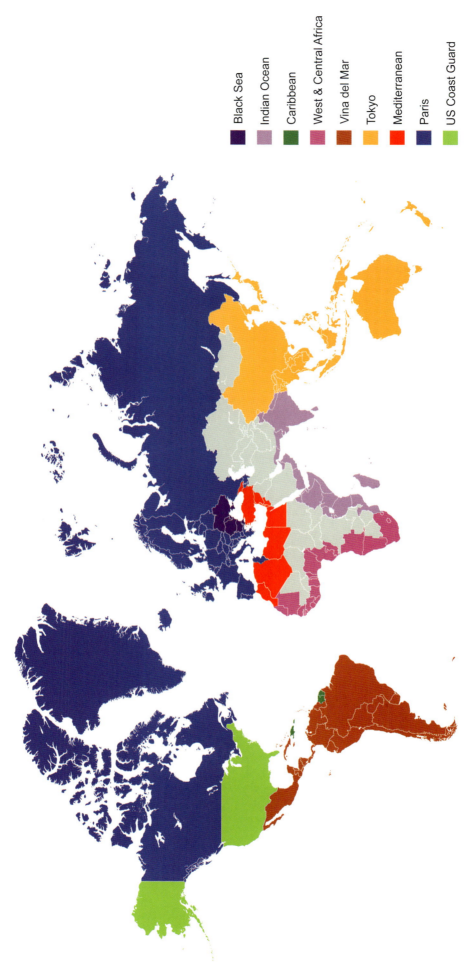

Figure 2.18: The different Port State Control MOU regions

Legend:
- Black Sea
- Indian Ocean
- Caribbean
- West & Central Africa
- Vina del Mar
- Tokyo
- Mediterranean
- Paris
- US Coast Guard

Failure to meet the necessary standards will lead to deficiencies that may need to be corrected before the ship's departure or within a certain time period and could even lead to the ship's detention.

2.5.4 Classification Societies and certification

Classification Societies are non-governmental bodies that provide rules to which the vast majority of commercial ships, and certain marine equipment, are designed and built. The Register Society was the first such organisation, publishing its Register of Ships in 1764. This gave interested parties, including underwriters and merchants, an idea of the condition of a vessel, which helped in assessing the risk of a particular venture. This organisation became Lloyd's Register of British and Foreign Shipping in 1834. Lloyd's Register (LR) now operates across many industry sectors, with some 9,000 employees based in 78 countries. There are now many other Classification Societies and the term 'in Class' refers to the fact that a ship is complying with the rules of a particular society.

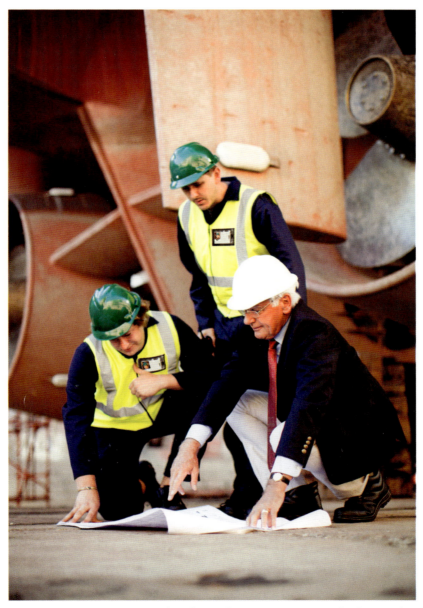

Figure 2.19: Class Societies provide rules and inspections to certify ships as 'in Class'

To ensure compliance with the rules, as well as other national and international statutory regulations that may apply, the Classification Society's surveyors will validate drawings and monitor the construction of new vessels. Regular surveys are then carried out during the life of a ship, either on a periodic basis or following major repairs or alterations, to ensure standards are maintained. Despite this, a Classification Society cannot guarantee the seaworthiness of a vessel since it has no control over manning, operation or maintenance between the periodical surveys that it conducts. Classification Societies usually act as Recognised Organisations (ROs) on behalf of a Flag State by carrying out surveys and issuing or endorsing statutory certificates in accordance with the RO Code (Code for Recognized Organizations). ROs also cooperate with Port State Control Administrations, such as the MCA, to ensure detection and correction of any deficiencies or discrepancies.

2.6 The Role of the European Union

Figure 2.20: The EU flag and headquarters in Brussels

2.6.1 The European Commission and Parliament

Around 90% of European Union external trade is by sea and short sea shipping, or coastal shipping, representing 40% of internal trade movements in terms of ton-kilometres. In addition, some 400 million passengers embark and disembark in European ports each year. The European Commission (EC) has strict safety rules to prevent sub-standard shipping, to reduce the risk of maritime accidents and to minimise the environmental impact of shipping in its waters. EC work in the maritime sector also includes combatting piracy and terrorism, seafarers' working conditions and professional qualifications and the rights of passengers. The part of the Commission responsible for these policy areas is the Directorate General for Mobility and Transport (DG MOVE). Separately, the Directorate General for Maritime Affairs and Fisheries (DG MARE) is responsible for fisheries and maritime policy – principally conservation, spatial planning and economic growth – within European waters.

Figure 2.21: The EU Parliament in Brussels

For ships on international voyages, the EC, in taking a role as regional legislator, inevitably adds a layer of regulation to that already required under international conventions. Where such additional rules apply to ships, they can add costs and decrease the competitiveness of EU shipping compared to other international operators.

EU shipping regulation is drafted by the European Commission and refined and approved by European Members of Parliament and then by the European Council – this is known as the trialogue procedure.

Following a referendum in June 2016, the UK voted to leave the European Union; this process formally began with the triggering of Article 50 in March 2017. Over the next two years, discussions will take place to negotiate the UK's exit and to outline their future relationship with the European Union. The effect that this will have on shipping and maritime legislation is currently unknown.

2.6.2   European Maritime Safety Agency (EMSA)

EMSA is a decentralised agency of the EU based in Lisbon. It provides technical support to the EC and to Member States on maritime safety, pollution and security, and has operational roles for oil pollution response, vessel monitoring and long-range identification and tracking (LRIT) of ships. The Agency operates a number of stand-by oil recovery vessels to assist Member States in the event of pollution.

Figure 2.22: EMSA provides technical support to EU Member States, who then enforce legislation in inspections

The organisation was founded in 2002 following major losses in European waters, notably the cruise-ferry *'Estonia'* and the oil tankers *'Erika'* and *'Prestige'*, when it was felt that a specialised technical agency was necessary to manage the development and enforcement of legislation.

Key Point Summary

1) Shipping is one of the most global industries, necessitating regulation at an international level.

2) MARPOL and SOLAS have led to the adoption of international regulation that has greatly improved the safety of ships and reduced incidents of pollution.

3) The registration of a vessel to a particular Flag State obliges that State to survey and inspect the vessel for regulatory compliance. The survey and inspection of a vessel is often assigned to a Classification Society.

4) Enforcement is also achieved through Port State Control, whereby inspections are carried out to ensure the compliance of ships visiting foreign ports.

5) Certification provides documentary evidence that a vessel is compliant with international regulation and has been surveyed accordingly.

6) The IMO is key to developing internationally agreed codes and conventions, but effective enforcement is critical to maintaining standards.

Regulation of UK Ships

3.1   Introduction

This chapter looks at how the UK interprets and implements international shipping regulations, introducing the various UK regulatory agencies involved in shipping, and discusses the legal and administrative processes relevant to working and operating a British flagged or owned ship. It examines the processes involved in flagging a ship in the UK and securing the certificates required in order to trade. Historically, a shipowner would register their ship in the State where they were based. However, this national connection was lost in the early part of the 20th century. The decision of where to register a vessel is one of the most important a shipowner will take. This chapter looks at some of the considerations that an owner will need to assess when making this decision, as well as some of the reasons why they might choose the UK as their register.

3.2   Flagging

Figure 3.1: Ships passing the Strait of Dover, one of Britain's principal shipping routes

3.2.1   The process of flagging in the UK

Owners and bareboat charterers who wish to register their vessels on the UK Ship Register (UKSR) must satisfy a number of criteria. They must be a citizen of the UK, a British dependent territory, a British overseas territory or a Member State of the EU. Alternatively, they may be a company incorporated in a British overseas territory that has its principal place of business in the UK, a British dependent or overseas territory, or an EU Member State. If none of the qualified owners are resident in the UK, a representative must be appointed who is either an individual resident in the UK or a company incorporated in one of the European Economic Area (EEA) countries with a place of business in the UK.

There are several advantages of registering to the UK flag. It meets the Paris MoU flag criteria for low risk ships, so UK ships are less frequently targeted for Port State Control inspections. Statutory surveys (except ISM, ISPS and MLC) for eligible non-passenger vessels are delegated to Classification Societies without a formal appointment under the Alternative Compliance Scheme (ACS).

Ship registration costs £124 and there's a renewal fee of £49 every five years. By comparison, Panama has a once only registration fee, but it is charged at a rate per tonne that can end up being considerably more expensive. For example, a 20,000 GT vessel would require a one-off fee of $4,000. However, cost is only one consideration when choosing a register and there are many other factors to consider, the main ones of which are covered later in this chapter. A ship registered on the UKSR will receive a Certificate of British Registry that is subject to renewal every 5 years.

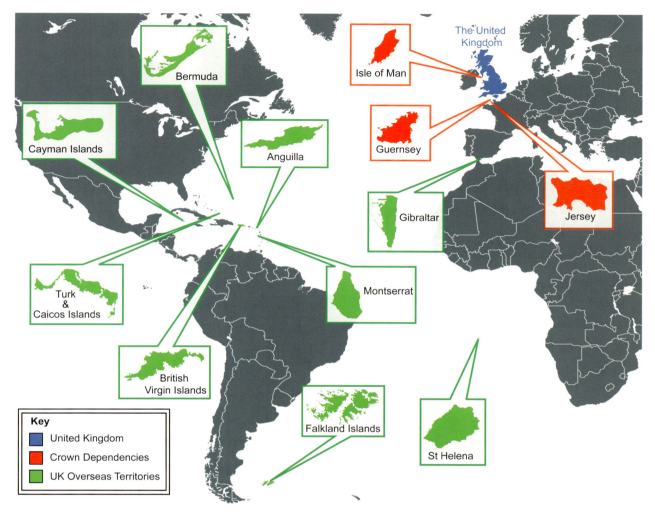

Figure 3.2: A map of the Red Ensign Group

Any vessel registered in the UK, a Crown Dependency or a UK Overseas Territory is a 'British ship' and is entitled to fly the Red Ensign. Merchant vessels from British Overseas Territories and Crown Dependencies are entitled to Red Ensigns overlaid with the insignia of their territory. The Red Ensign Group (REG) is a group of British Shipping Registers made up by the following:

- The United Kingdom

- The Crown Dependencies

  » Isle of Man

  » Guernsey

  » Jersey

- The UK Overseas Territories

  » Anguilla

  » Bermuda

  » British Virgin Islands

  » Cayman Islands

  » Falkland Islands

  » Gibraltar

  » Montserrat

  » St Helena

  » Turks & Caicos Islands.

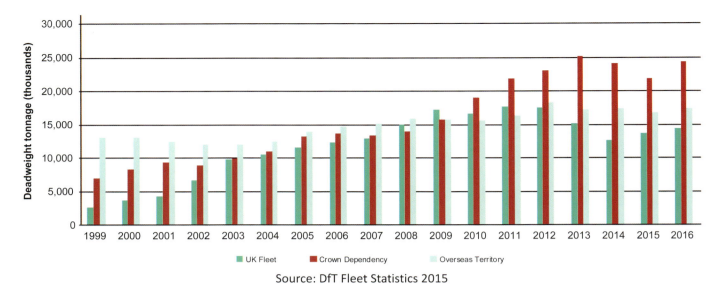

Source: DfT Fleet Statistics 2015

Figure 3.3: The Red Ensign Group registered trading vessels, 100 GT and over, 1999–2016

The combined Red Ensign Group fleet represented a total of 43.2 million GT in 2015, making the group the seventh largest Flag State in the world by GT and equal to 3.7% of global tonnage. Under the United Nations Convention on the Law of the Sea (UNCLOS), all ships registered within the Crown Dependencies and British Overseas Territories are British Ships. The United Kingdom, as the Flag State for these ships, has devolved to the Crown Dependencies and British Overseas Territories the authority to carry out all Flag State responsibilities under IMO conventions. It permits these registries to set their own rules, while enabling operators to enjoy the benefits of security and prestige that the Red Ensign provides.

Figure 3.4: The Red Ensign at sea

3.2.2 Factors influencing shipowners' choice of flag

Shipowners do not necessarily have to register their ships in their country of residence (or business) and flagging is largely a commercial decision, influenced by:

- **Corporate custom.** A shipowner will have close contact with the Flag State administration responsible for the survey and certification of his ships. A good working relationship with the Administration and with its surveyors will encourage the shipowner to remain with that Flag State.

- **Vessel type.** Certain flags have a strong reputation in specific shipping sectors (e.g. the Bahamas for cruise ships) and have registry practices and rules tailored to these sectors.

- **Quality reputation.** Many shipowners seek to trade on a reputation for quality. The registration of ships under a flag that is recognised as upholding safety standards and being well run is an important element of a quality reputation.

- **Marketing.** As well as conferring an assurance of quality, a particular flag may have specific marketing benefits in some sectors. Several cruise lines and ferry companies promote a holiday/travel experience linked to the nationality of its customers.

- **Charterer specification.** The charter under which a ship is employed may stipulate the flag under which it must operate; a charterer is free, as a customer, to make any stipulation they wish. Quality assurance is a typical reason for stipulating a particular flag.

- **Bank specification.** The bank that finances the purchase of a ship will wish to ensure that it is operated and maintained to a high standard. It will also need to be reassured that the ship is registered in a jurisdiction where it is confident that a mortgage is good security and where payment terms can be enforced. Therefore, it may stipulate a group of acceptable flags to which a ship may be registered.

- **Shipyard specification.** Shipyards similarly have well-established relationships with particular Flag State administrations, building ships to the specifications of their surveyors. A standard contract may specify that the ship will be built to meet the requirements of a particular Flag State, with alternative flags available only at additional cost to cover the requirement for bespoke design or re-survey.

- **Cost of operation.** The cost of operating a ship under one flag may be greater than under another due to the application of domestic laws. The difference may be a matter of the direct cost of employing seafarers of prescribed nationalities or at prescribed rates of pay or other remuneration (e.g. pension entitlements), or of the indirect cost associated with the risk of legal proceedings at employment tribunals. Equally, it may be a matter of opportunity cost: marriages cannot be performed on UK-flagged ships, so all UK-flagged ships are excluded from providing onboard weddings in the cruise sector.

- **Access to flag-restricted cabotage trades.** A shipowner wishing to operate in the domestic trades of countries where flag-based access restrictions apply will need to register the ship appropriately. Examples include Brazil, Japan and the USA.

- **Insurance.** Underwriters may require that a ship is flagged in one of a group of flags that they consider to be acceptable.

- **Liability to requisition.** Registration under certain flags (for example the US and UK) renders the ship liable to requisition by the Flag State, while some States may be more likely than others to undertake military operations requiring the requisitioning of ships. This occurred during the Falklands War, when a variety of merchant navy ships were requisitioned as Ships Taken Up From Trade (STUFT).

- **Flag administration and survey costs.** These can vary significantly between Flag States.

- **Naval protection.** Some States offer naval protection to ships on their register and such protection is valuable where the ship is at risk of attack (whether by pirates or by another State).

Figure 3.5: The UK has one of the world's largest and most advanced navies, which offers considerable protection to global shipping

3.3   Statutory Liability Regimes

Shipowners are required to demonstrate to governments, port authorities and charterers that they have insurance cover in place for third party liabilities. The coverage of such insurance includes claims for pollution, personal injury and wreck removal.

Figure 3.6: P&I Clubs provide insurance against accidents at sea

This insurance is normally provided by Protection and Indemnity (P&I) Clubs and is evidenced by the issuance of insurance certificates known as certificates of entry. Certificates of entry are carried on board as evidence of the fact that the vessel is entered with a P&I Club.

Liability conventions exist to ensure compensation for damage resulting from different types of pollution that a ship can potentially cause. The conventions typically impose strict liability on shipowners, meaning that claimants do not need to prove that the shipowner was at fault. However, they place limits on the amounts that shipowners are liable to pay. Many of the conventions also require the shipowner to have insurance, as well as permitting direct action against the insurer. It is common for UK-registered ships and ships calling at UK ports to carry Flag State certificates ('Blue Cards') to prove that they have the relevant compulsory insurance against various types of pollution and other liability claims. The specific requirements depend on ship type and size.

For example, strict liability is imposed on the shipowner for any persistent oil (e.g. crude or residual) spilled as a result of its carriage as cargo. However, under the Civil Liability for Oil Pollution Damage Convention (CLC), insurance is only a necessity for ships carrying over 2,000 tonnes of persistent oil as cargo. Another example is where vessels are licensed to carry more than 12 passengers under a contract of carriage on international voyages and are either:

(a) registered to a ratifying Flag State

(b) calling or leaving a ratifying Port State.

In this circumstance, a Blue Card must be produced as evidence of insurance to meet their strict but capped liabilities to passengers and their luggage in the event of an incident, in accordance with the 2002 Protocol to the Athens Convention.

3.4 Certification in the UK

3.4.1 Attaining Class

All seagoing vessels registered in the UK are assigned to a specific ship Class. This defines a ship's permitted use and the certificates it must hold, and specifies the applicable inspection and survey regime for demonstrating compliance with certification requirements. The Classes are established and assigned by the recognised Classification Societies, which also carry out ship surveys and inspections. Statutory certificates (except ISM DOC, SMC and ISSC) are often issued by the Classification Society. Within the UK, the MCA seeks to streamline the survey and certification process by delegating all survey work to authorised Classification Societies through the Alternative Compliance Scheme. This scheme is available to all vessels that trade internationally, except passenger ships. Certain eligibility criteria have to be met (for example, a vessel that has been detained within the preceding 36 months or has had more than 5 deficiencies recorded in the previous 12 months is not eligible). Survey procedures and dates for all major ship certificates are harmonised according to the Harmonized System of Survey and Certification (HSSC) developed by the IMO.

Figure 3.7: Class inspectors check, among other things, the hull and ship's equipment

The certificates that must be carried for UK-registered vessels vary according to a vessel's type, gross tonnage, the type of cargo carried and whether they are on a domestic or international voyage. An outline of the main certification requirements is included as Annex 1, but two examples are:

- The passenger ship safety certificate:

  » Required for all passenger ships that carry more than 12 passengers

  » Requires an annual survey

  » Covers the SOLAS requirements of ship stability and construction, the state of the hull, machinery, fire-fighting equipment, life-saving appliances and navigation and radio equipment

- The safe manning document:

  » Ensures that ships are manned with personnel of appropriate grades who have been properly trained and certificated

  » Specific requirements for safe manning are laid down in Regulation 14 of Chapter V SOLAS to ensure navigational safety

  » The numbers of certificated officers and certificated and non-certificated ratings must be sufficient to ensure safe and efficient operation of the ship at all times.

3.4.2   Class suspension

Class may be suspended either automatically or following the decision of the Classification Society.

Class may be suspended automatically for a number of reasons, such as:

- A ship not operating in compliance with the rule requirements

- Trading outside the navigation restrictions for which the Class was assigned

- Proceeding to sea with less freeboard than that assigned

- The owner failing to inform the Class Society after defects or damages affecting the Class have been detected.

It will also be suspended automatically if the Class renewal survey has not been completed by its limit date or when the annual or intermediate surveys have not been completed by the end of the corresponding survey time window.

Figure 3.8: In some extreme cases, a Classification Society may suspend Class following an inspection, and reports are then made to the Flag and Port States

Class of a ship may also be suspended following the decision of the society, for example when a recommendation is not dealt with within the time limit specified. Suspension will remain in place until the issue in question has been resolved. Until that time, the vessel will be unable to trade. If, however, the causes that have given rise to a suspension have not been removed within six months, Class will normally be withdrawn. For that vessel to trade again, it would have to start the entire Classification process again. Withdrawal of Class more normally occurs when a ship is lost, is a constructive loss or is reported as scrapped. The vessel will then be deleted from the Register of Ships.

3.5 Regulation and Marine Administration in the UK

3.5.1 UK Government

Governance and regulation of shipping in UK waters is primarily devolved to the Shipping Minister, traditionally a junior Minister within the Department for Transport (DfT). In Scotland, it is devolved to the Scottish Minister for Transport and his department, Marine Scotland. Shipping is also subject to regulation from other Government departments, including the Department for Environment, Food and Rural Affairs (DEFRA), the Home Office (for security and border control issues) and HM Treasury (UK taxation including VAT). Other Government departments also provide advice and guidance to the industry, including the Ministry of Defence (piracy and other maritime security and defence related subjects) and the Foreign and Commonwealth Office (piracy and other diplomatic issues).

Figure 3.9: The Palace of Westminster

3.5.2 The Merchant Shipping Act 1995

The UK's Merchant Shipping Act 1995 is the central Act of Parliament governing shipping. It covers a wide range of shipping-related regulations including registrations of ships, use of ensigns, safety and pollution matters, the function of lighthouse authorities and enforcement. It updated the Merchant Shipping Act 1894 and unified much of the nation's maritime legislation. It repealed some Acts, and amended provisions in others, some of which dated back to the mid-19th century. More recently, amendments to it were enacted through the Marine Navigation Act 2013. This primary legislation is supported by secondary legislation, brought into force by means of Statutory Instruments (SIs). As well as domestic legislation devised by the government, Merchant Shipping Notices (MSNs) may also bring into force the provisions contained in international conventions once they have been ratified by the UK.

3.5.3   The Maritime and Coastguard Agency (MCA)

As an agency of the UK's Department for Transport (DfT), the Maritime and Coastguard Agency (MCA) is the regulatory and inspection authority for all UK shipping. Based in Southampton, head office policy staff provide guidance on the interpretation and implementation of legislation, both domestic and international. Regional surveyors, situated in marine offices in major ports around the UK, undertake inspections of ships either to ensure compliance with Flag State requirements for ships on the UK register or to conduct Port State Control inspections of foreign vessels. The MCA is also responsible for the certification of UK seafarers. As such, it ensures that courses attended by trainee officers conform to the requirements of STCW and, following successful written and oral MCA examinations, it will issue the appropriate certificates of competency.

Figure 3.10: HM Coastguard coordinate British search and rescue

HM Coastguard is also a part of the MCA. In total, there are around 1,050 staff and 3,500 volunteers who are responsible for all civilian maritime search and rescue (SAR) within the UK. This ranges from individuals who may be having difficulties on the cliffs to a merchant ship facing an emergency at sea within the UK Maritime Search and Rescue Region, which extends far into the Atlantic. Activity is coordinated from a number of Maritime Rescue Coordination Centres (MRCC) and a single National Maritime Operations Centre (NMOC) in Fareham, Hampshire.

As the UK's maritime authority, the MCA acts as the regulator of shipping in the UK in addition to fulfilling a number of international obligations. These include:

- Safety of people and vessels in UK waters

- Safety of seafarers on all UK-flagged vessels

- Provision of weather broadcasts and maritime safety information delivered by HM Coastguard to ships via NAVTEX, VHF and MF

- Maintenance of the UK Ship Register and the conduct of Flag State surveys

- Ensuring marine equipment meets the required performance standards through the appointment of Recognised Organisations

- Environmental safety of the UK coast and waters and response to pollution incidents.

Key

▲ UK Search and Rescue Helicopter Base

◎ Coastguard Operations Centre

Figure 3.11: UK SAR provision

3.5.4 UK Port State Control

Port State Control (PSC) is an internationally agreed regime for the inspection of foreign ships in other national ports by PSC inspectors. The intent is to ensure compliance with the requirements of international conventions, such as SOLAS, MARPOL, STCW and the MLC. In response to the variable performance of Flag States in fulfilling this compliance, a number of European countries agreed in 1982 upon a supplementary regime of PSC, established in the Paris MoU. This has helped to ensure a more consistent and thorough inspection regime throughout Europe. Other groups of countries have set up comparable arrangements, which are listed in Chapter 2.

Within the UK, the MCA is responsible for PSC. Merchant shipping notice (MSN) 1832 sets out the guidance for UK PSC, including ship risk profiles, frequency and scope of inspections, reporting requirements for ships and procedures relating to detentions.

Figure 3.12: The MCA oversees PSC in the UK

Expanded inspections are carried out on vessels with high risk profiles (as recorded on the Paris MoU database) and vessels over 12 years old in the following categories:

- Oil, gas and chemical tankers

- Bulk carriers

- Passenger ships.

Masters of these vessels must give the MCA 72 hours' notice prior to arrival in a UK port.

3.5.5 Marine Accident Investigation Branch (MAIB)

Source: MAIB

Figure 3.13: The UK MAIB investigates marine accidents and produces reports, such as on the *'Hoegh Osaka'* grounding in 2015

The Marine Accident Investigation Branch is charged with investigating accidents involving UK vessels worldwide and all vessels in UK waters. According to its website, it receives between 1,500 and 1,800 accident reports each year on accidents of all types and severity, resulting in about 30 investigation reports being produced. It is based in Southampton, is an independent department within the Department for Transport and has a staff of about 35. It is not an enforcement or prosecuting body, but rather seeks to improve safety standards and awareness at sea by the publication of full and detailed reports that can be accessed via their website. MGN 458 sets out all the requirements for reporting accidents.

3.5.6 Marine notices

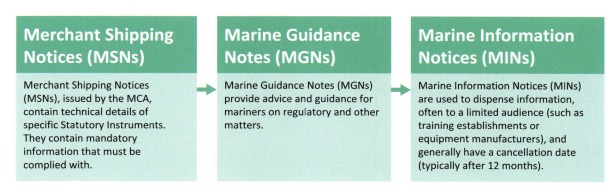

Marine notices contain regulatory information and guidance for seafarers, ship managers, superintendents and marine personnel. Generically, MSNs, MGNs and MINs are called Marine Notices and suffixes may be used to indicate their relevance to merchant ships (M), fishing vessels (F), or both (M+F). Masters and ships' officers will need to be familiar with their content and, where relevant, M Notices will need to be carried on board.

3.5.7 UK Hydrographic Office (UKHO)

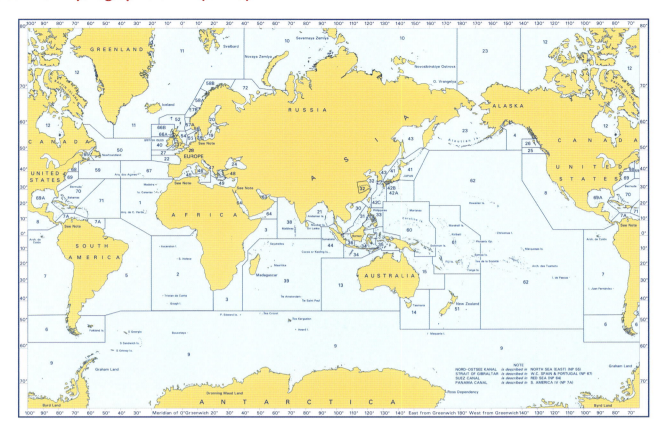

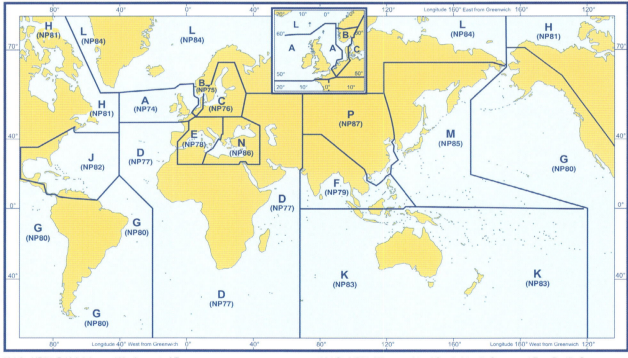

Vol A - NP74 British Isles and North coast of France

Vol B - NP75 Southern and Eastern sides of the North Sea

Vol C - NP76 Baltic Sea

Vol D - NP77 Eastern Atlantic Ocean, Western Indian Ocean, Arabian and Red Seas

Vol E - NP78 West Mediterranean

Vol F - NP79 North-East Indian Ocean, Central part of South China and Eastern Archipelagic Seas (North of the Equator), excluding China, and South-West part of Philippine Sea

Vol G - NP80 Western side of South Atlantic Ocean and East Pacific Ocean

Vol H - NP81 Northern and Eastern coasts of Canada

Vol J - NP82 Western side of North Atlantic Ocean

Vol K - NP83 Indian and Pacific Oceans, south of the Equator

Vol L - NP84 Northern Seas

Vol M - NP85 Western side of North Pacific Ocean

Vol N - NP86 East Mediterranean and Black Seas

Vol P - NP87 North part of South China and Eastern Archipelagic Seas, plus Western part of East China, Philippine and Yellow Seas, including Taiwan Strait and Eastern part of Gulf of Tonkin

Figure 3.14: The UKHO provides charts and sailing publications to ships for safe navigation

Under SOLAS, contracting governments are obliged to chart their own territorial waters and ensure the provision of relevant hydrographic and nautical services. For the UK, this function is carried out by the UKHO, which provides commercial shipping with the navigational charts and other hydrographic information (such as sailing directions, lists of lights and tide tables) required for compliance with international regulations, defence and other national hydrographic offices. UKHO and other national hydrographic offices also issue Notices to Mariners (NMs) as well as Radio Navigational Warnings to alert vessels to matters affecting navigational safety. These documents, where relevant to the intended voyage, will need to be carried on board, either in hard copy or electronic format, in order to meet carriage requirements.

3.5.8   Crown Estate

The Crown Estate is a property portfolio owned by the State. It is one of the largest property owners in the UK with assets worth more than £8.1bn. It owns almost all of the seabed out to 12 nautical miles off the UK coast and has the rights to generate electricity from wind, tidal and wave energy on the Continental Shelf. Licensing of offshore windfarms and tidal/wave farms has been a highly contentious issue in recent years, especially when the facilities are sited in or adjacent to important shipping lanes.

3.5.9   Marine Management Organisation

The Marine Management Organisation (MMO) is an executive non-departmental public body in the UK established under the Marine and Coastal Access Act (MCAA) 2009. The MMO exists to make a significant contribution to sustainable development in the marine area and to promote the UK's vision for clean, healthy, safe, productive and biologically diverse oceans and seas. Its powers enable it to set up a marine planning system and a marine licensing regime (required for pipelines, dredging operations etc.). It also manages the UK fishing fleet capacity and the UK fisheries quotas.

The organisation works with Natural England and the Joint Nature Conservation Committee (JNCC) to create and manage a network of marine protected areas (Marine Conservation Zones and European Marine Sites) designed to preserve vulnerable habitats and species in UK marine waters. It also responds to marine emergencies alongside other agencies, and has developed an internationally recognised centre of excellence for marine information that supports its decision making process.

Key Point Summary

1) There are several advantages to registering a vessel in the UK, but the decision of where to register is influenced by numerous factors dependent on the owner's/operator's business.

2) UK-registered ships and ships arriving at or departing from ports in the UK, must have Flag State certificates to prove they have the relevant compulsory civil liability insurance cover, including against oil pollution and wrecks.

3) All seagoing vessels registered in the UK are assigned to a specific ship Class, which defines their permitted use. Ships must comply with the national certification requirements and failure can result in Class suspension and ship detention.

4) International regulation is transposed into UK law in addition to any specific regulatory requirements of the UK Government. These are regulated by a number of different Government departments and agencies.

Crewing and Employment

4.1   Introduction

Any shipping company establishing itself in the UK will need to engage crews in order to operate its ships. The crews will need to be made up of competent, qualified seafarers who are capable of fulfilling each voyage in a safe and timely manner. The company will need sufficient numbers for each voyage, along with reserve officers and crew in the event that a voyage is so lengthy as to require crew members to be relieved after a certain period of time at sea. The company will also require cover for unforeseen absences such as sickness.

There may be restrictions as to the nationalities of crew members employed. All officers, whatever their nationality, will need to be qualified in line with international standards of competency and hold valid Certificates of Competency (CoCs). If they trained in a country other than the UK, they will need to obtain Certificates of Equivalent Competency, which attest that the standards of competency required for their CoC are equivalent to those required by the UK.

The company has a duty to ensure that all crew members are familiar with the ship before embarking on a voyage and know what to do in an emergency. It will also need to ensure that its crews are capable of putting into practice the company's safety management system (SMS).

The company must take account of the Maritime Labour Convention, 2006 (MLC). Commonly described as the seafarers' bill of rights, this international convention provides seafarers of all nationalities and ranks with a variety of rights relating to their living and working conditions on board.

The company will also need to be aware of certain domestic employment laws that cover all shore-based workers in the UK and may apply to some or all of their crews. In addition, it will want to avoid incurring unnecessary costs by arranging for crew members to be employed by an overseas company, which minimises the liability for employers' National Insurance Contributions (NICs). UK seafarers will find it more attractive to work on a ship that enables them to spend at least 183 days in a year outside the UK, as they will not be charged income tax on their earnings as seafarers under the Seafarers' Earnings Deduction scheme (SED).

Figure 4.1: To work on a ship, deck officers and crew are required to learn the key principles of navigation, including keeping charts up to date

4.2   Roles on Board, Safe Manning and the Role of the Master

Most ships will have:

- A Master, who has overall responsibility for the ship

- A Chief Officer, who leads the deck department (including navigation)

- Deck officers, who are responsible for carrying out a watch both in port and at sea

- A Chief Engineer, who is in charge of the engine room team responsible for the ship's machinery

- Engineers, who are responsible for maintaining and operating the ship's machinery

- A cook, who is tasked with providing the crew with food

- A bosun or chief petty officer (CPO), who supervises the ratings

- Ratings, including able seamen (AB), ordinary seamen (OS) and trainees.

Courtesy of Danny Cornelissen

Figure 4.2: Examples of crew that can be found on board

Some ships carry trainee seafarers, who are not part of the ship's crew but are on board to gain experience and develop their competencies. These may include deck, Electro-Technical Officer (ETO) and engine cadets who are studying towards becoming officers and follow a set schedule of training to achieve qualifications.

The Master's role is quite complex. Not only is the Master an employee of the shipowner, they are also the employer's representative on board and an agent of the shipowner, and so can act and negotiate on the shipowner's behalf in situations where this is necessary. The Master is the bailee of any cargo being carried by the ship, meaning that they are legally in possession of the cargo once it has been delivered on board, even though they are not the owner. As such, the Master is responsible for the cargo's safe carriage until it is discharged from the ship.

The Master can act as an agent of necessity, meaning that they have implied powers to act in the best interests of persons and property on board a ship that is in peril. This could involve entering into a contract with a salvor on behalf of the ship's owner. Instructions will come from the shipowner and also from the charterer if the ship is on charter. The Master may also be instructed by Flag State surveyors and Port State Control officers.

Every ship over 500 GT requires a Safe Manning Document (SMD), which is issued by the Flag State authority. Normally, the company will make a proposal for the minimum personnel required on the ship to operate it in compliance with all applicable regulations. This will cover not only the overall crew size, but the number of officers required in the navigating and engineering departments. The national competent authority (the MCA in the UK) will either approve the company's proposal or require greater numbers of personnel than shown. It is an offence to put the ship to sea with less than the specified minimum manning, although in emergency cases the competent authority may grant a dispensation for a particular voyage. In general, ships will have an 'operational' manning level in excess of the minimum stated on the SMD.

Passenger ships will typically carry a large number of 'hotel' staff to provide services for passengers. On a cruise ship, this will include waiters, cabin stewards, shopkeepers, hairdressers, musicians, fitness instructors and croupiers.

4.3   Crew Nationality

The ship's Flag State may make rules concerning the nationalities of the crew members employed on board. Some States reserve the positions of Master and other senior officers for their own nationals, although restrictions in respect of other crew members are rare if a ship trades internationally. A 'strategic' ship registered in the UK is required to employ a Master who is a national of the UK, or of any other EEA, Commonwealth or NATO member country. Strategic ships are ships of 500 GT or more that are cruise ships, product tankers, RoRo ships or fishing vessels of 24 metres or more in length. Aside from this provision, nationality is no barrier to employment on board a UK ship – unless the ship is subject to the points-based system for entry into the UK for employment (see Section 4.6 of this chapter).

4.4   Entry into Employment: the STCW Regime

To serve as an officer on a merchant ship, a Certificate of Competency (CoC) must be obtained by meeting the standards of competence for the role set out in the International Convention on Standards of Training, Certification and Watchkeeping (the STCW Convention). There are two qualification levels for officers in the deck and engine departments. In the deck department, the junior level is the Officer of the Watch (OOW) and the senior qualifications are from a Chief Mate CoC to a Master CoC. In the engine room, the junior level is the Engineer OOW and the senior levels are from Second Engineer to Chief Engineer. Variations apply to deck CoCs restricted to service on ships of less than 500 GT and/or operating solely on near-coastal voyages[1] and to engine CoCs restricted to ships with propulsion power under 750 kW and 3,000 kW.

Under the UK training regime, it takes three years for a person to attain their CoC as OOW in the deck department and three years for an Engineer OOW. The training encompasses a combination of time spent on board ship in a supernumerary capacity and time undertaking academic and practical study at a maritime college (and, for trainee engineers, practical training in a workshop). Trainees are usually sponsored by shipping companies, some of whom operate their own training schemes and aim to provide sea time on board their ships. However, most shipping companies have arrangements with training management companies who administer training on their behalf. Companies meet the costs of training and

---

[1] Defined in the STCW Convention as voyages in the vicinity of a party to the Convention, as defined by that party. The UK defines near-coastal voyages for UK-registered ships as those extending no more than 60 nautical miles from a safe haven in the UK.

maintenance of their sponsored trainees, although the costs may be partially offset via the Government's scheme of Support for Maritime Training (SMarT).

Figure 4.3: Cadets train at approved maritime colleges and graduate following extensive training both at college and at sea

CoCs are also available for electro-technical officers, who are responsible for maintaining the proper functioning of the ship's electrical systems. Certificates of Proficiency are awarded to ratings forming part of a navigational or engine room watch, electro-technical ratings and able seafarers on completion of the requisite sea service and/or approved training. There is no specific STCW qualification for a ship's cook or others working in a ship's catering department.

Figure 4.4: A Certificate of Competency is awarded to an officer who has met the standards set out in STCW and is mandatory for service on board a ship

Officers who hold CoCs issued by national administrations other than the UK will be required to obtain Certificates of Equivalent Competency (CECs) in order to be permitted to serve as officers on ships registered in the UK. If the standard of competency necessary to obtain their original CoC falls short of the UK requirements, they will need to undertake assessments to ensure that they reach the UK standards. The competency standards required for CoCs issued by all EEA Member States are equivalent to the UK standards.

Applicants will also need to demonstrate an adequate knowledge of the English language, via a specific language test if necessary. Officers seeking a CEC at Master/Chief Mate/Chief Engineer level will also be required to pass an examination in UK legal and administrative processes.

All seafarers, including hotel services staff, must undertake shipboard safety and security familiarisation, and security awareness training, before the commencement of their voyage. Those with safety and/or security duties must also complete courses in basic safety and security training. Safety training includes training or instruction in personal survival techniques, fire prevention and fire-fighting, elementary first aid and personal safety and social responsibilities.

There are additional special training requirements for personnel working on oil and chemical tankers or on passenger ships.

4.5   Global Standards: Maritime Labour Convention, 2006

4.5.1   Background

The Maritime Labour Convention, 2006 (MLC) is an international treaty that consolidated more than 70 different instruments covering a variety of topics related to seafaring employment, with the aim of bringing them into effect worldwide. It has become known as the seafarers' bill of rights and is the fourth pillar of international regulation for global shipping, alongside the IMO conventions SOLAS, MARPOL and STCW.

The MLC was developed by the International Labour Organization (ILO), which, like the IMO, is an agency of the United Nations. Founded in 1919, it set out to establish minimum standards for conditions of employment and, in 1920, it established a process to develop instruments specific to the maritime sector. This was to address concerns that seafarers, as a result of the transnational nature of their work, might miss out on important workplace rights and protections that land-based workers benefit from.

Courtesy of Danny Cornelissen

Figure 4.5: The MLC regulates seafarer employment rights, living and working conditions, and safety standards

The ILO has a unique tripartite structure that gives voting rights to representatives of employers and employees from each participating country. This contrasts with other UN agencies in which only governments may vote. The effect of this is that employer and employee representatives are able to set the agenda for discussions and seek to reach agreement between themselves. Specific to the maritime industry, the ILO has adopted conventions and recommendations covering such matters as compensation for seafarers in the event of sickness or injury, health and safety and accident prevention, food and catering on board, repatriation of seafarers, employment agreements, crew accommodation on board and working hours.

Unfortunately for the seafarers, few of these conventions attracted sufficient ratifications to become truly effective and many did not enter into force. An attempt was made to implement some of the most important provisions through the adoption of the Merchant Shipping (Minimum Standards) Convention, 1976 (No. 147). This encouraged countries to adopt measures that were substantially equivalent to the key employment and health and safety protection measures, which, for the first time in an ILO convention, allowed countries to inspect ships visiting their ports to ensure compliance with the standards. This was the first ILO maritime convention to cover more than 50% of the world fleet. However, its standards were not uniform and there was no provision for its enforcement by Flag States.

Shipowner and seafarer representatives agreed, in 2001, to bring the key provisions of each measure together into one single instrument, with enforcement mechanisms for Flag States, Port States and seafarers themselves to ensure compliance with the minimum requirements. This became the Maritime Labour Convention, 2006 (MLC).

The MLC entered into force globally on 20th August 2013 and, as of May 2017, more than 90% of ships in the world fleet were registered in States that had ratified the MLC.

4.5.2   MLC structure

The structure of the MLC is modelled on the STCW Convention and is unlike any other ILO convention. It contains articles, which provide the legal base; regulations, which set out the requirements in broad terms; and a code, which is divided into two sections: Part A, containing mandatory provisions and Part B, containing non-mandatory guidance.

4.5.3 The articles

Article II contains the definitions of seafarer, ship and shipowner, which are crucial to determining who the MLC applies to. A provision allows individual governments to decide whether a particular type of vessel is a ship and a particular person working on board is a seafarer in cases where there is doubt. Ships of traditional build, such as dhows and junks, fishing vessels, warships and naval auxiliaries are not included. Ships that are ordinarily engaged in commercial activities are included, unless they navigate exclusively in inland waters or waters within, or closely adjacent to, sheltered waters or areas where port regulations apply. The meaning of sheltered waters is for individual States to determine.

As a result, the MLC applies to large commercial yachts that are, at any time, made available for charter. It may also cover mobile offshore units with their own independent means of propulsion.

The default definition of seafarer is anyone employed, engaged or working on a ship to which the MLC applies. However, it has been agreed that maritime pilots are not covered and neither are surveyors carrying out inspections on behalf of a Flag or Port State authority. On some offshore support vessels, exclusions have been granted for charterer's personnel who work on the business of the charterer rather than of the ship. In addition, most States have agreed that privately contracted armed security personnel, who are hired to provide protection for ships and their crews from pirate attacks, are not to be considered as seafarers. This is principally because to do so would make it difficult for them to be carried on ships where, for example, there were insufficient cabins to accommodate them, potentially leaving the ship and crew to sail unprotected.

Figure 4.6: Shipowners must provide a safe working environment on board their ships

The definition of shipowner is modelled on, but is not identical to, the definition of a company in the International Safety Management (ISM) Code. Its purpose is to ensure that, irrespective of which persons or organisations are directly responsible for performing particular functions in relation to a seafarer's employment, the seafarer always has recourse to the entity designated as the shipowner. The shipowner, meanwhile, cannot respond to a claim from a seafarer by stating that the subject matter of the claim is the responsibility of another person or entity. In many cases, the shipowner for MLC purposes will also be the ship's ISM company, but it may also be the owner, manager or bareboat charterer if they have assumed responsibility for the operation of the ship.

Article V contains a provision designed to encourage ratification of the MLC by requiring that States do not treat a ship visiting one of its ports and flying the Flag of a non-party more favourably than a visiting ship whose Flag State has ratified the MLC.

Article VI provides important clarification of the status of Parts A and B of the MLC Code and permits States not in a position to implement the rights and principles of Part A to meet the Convention's requirements by implementing measures that are substantially equivalent to the requirements. Article VI also requires that States take due account of the non-mandatory guidance in Part B when implementing Part A – ensuring that Part B cannot be ignored.

4.5.4 The Regulations and Code

The Regulations and the Code are divided into five 'titles', each covering particular themes:

Regulations and the Code	
	Title 1: Minimum requirements for seafarers to work on a ship
	Title 2: Conditions of employment
	Title 3: Accommodation, recreational facilities, food and catering
	Title 4: Health protection, medical care, welfare and social security protection
	Title 5: Compliance and enforcement.

Table 4.1: Regulations and the Code

Title 1: Minimum requirements for seafarers to work on a ship

This establishes the minimum age for seafarers to work on board a ship, which at the time of entry into force was set at 16 years. It requires that seafarers hold a valid medical certificate before commencing duty and outlines the processes that Flag States must follow in the medical examinations of seafarers. The maximum period of validity of a medical certificate is set at two years.

Title 1 also states that seafarers must be trained, certified as competent or otherwise qualified to perform their duties. Where appropriate, this will be met by training and certification carried out in accordance with the STCW Convention.

Figure 4.7: Seafarer rights and onboard conditions are covered by the MLC

Finally, Title 1 stipulates that recruitment and placement agencies supplying seafarers shall be licensed or otherwise regulated and sets out particular requirements. Agencies whose core business is not the supply of seafarers, or that supply only a small number of seafarers, are excluded, as are union hiring halls established by collective agreements. The key requirements are that services must be provided at no cost to seafarers and there is a prohibition on measures that prevent seafarers from gaining employment or deter employers from hiring them.

Title 2: Conditions of employment

Title 2 contains minimum requirements for seafarers' employment agreements, particulars of employment and provisions to ensure that seafarers have an opportunity to read and understand any such document before committing themselves to it. It requires that seafarers' wages are paid at regular intervals. Part B of the Code makes reference to the ILO recommended minimum monthly basic wage for an Able Seafarer.

Title 2 requires seafarers to be provided with minimum rest of 10 hours in any 24 hour period and 77 hours in any seven day period. The 10 hours may be divided into no more than two periods and one of these must be at least six hours. Every ship must have a table showing the schedule of duties for each seafarer and the shipowner must maintain records of the hours worked by each crew member, which must be made available for inspection. The schedule may be suspended by the Master in the event that the ship is in immediate danger or is assisting another ship or persons in danger. In addition, the competent authority may grant exceptions to the minima under national laws or regulations or by approving collective agreements that provide for different arrangements.

Title 2 provides seafarers with a minimum of 30 days' annual leave with pay, calculated on the basis of a minimum of 2.5 days per month of employment. It also sets out the seafarer's right to repatriation and makes provision for repatriation to be funded by Port States in the case of abandonment. Port States will then have the right to reclaim costs incurred from the relevant Flag State authorities. An amendment that took effect in January 2017 requires that shipowners provide financial security to ensure seafarers are repatriated in the event that they are abandoned by the shipowner.

Figure 4.8: Where risks to the health and safety of seafarers cannot be avoided, for example in noisy engine rooms, seafarers must be provided with personal protective equipment (PPE)

Title 2 also contains provision for seafarers to be compensated in the event of the ship's loss or foundering and a requirement that the ship's manning levels shall be adequate and take account of the IMO Principles of Safe Manning and concerns relating to seafarer fatigue.

Title 3: Accommodation, recreational facilities, food and catering

Title 3 requires that ships maintain decent accommodation and recreational facilities for seafarers. The requirements of the Convention apply to new ships[2]. For ships constructed before that date, ILO Conventions 92 and 133 shall continue to apply, to the extent that they already do apply. Specific provisions of the MLC include a requirement for a minimum headroom of

---

[2] A ship whose keel is laid, or is at a similar stage of construction, once the MLC has entered into force in the country whose flag it will fly.

203 cm in accommodation spaces, single-berth cabins for all seafarers not on passenger ships or special purpose ships and minimum provisions as to floor space.

Title 3 further requires that ships carry adequate food and drinking water supplies and that seafarers working on board are provided with food free of charge. A ship's cooks are required to complete approved training courses covering practical cookery, food and personal hygiene, food storage, stock control, environmental protection and catering health and safety. On a ship with fewer than 10 seafarers, a ship's cook may not be necessary, provided there is a crew member trained in food hygiene and food handling and storage on board ship. The minimum age for a ship's cook is 18 years.

Figure 4.9: An example of onboard living conditions (crew lounge, mess room, crew cabin and laundry room)

Title 4: Health protection, medical care, welfare and social security protection

Title 4 requires Port States to provide access to shoreside medical facilities for seafarers in cases of medical emergency and makes provisions for ships' medicine chests, ships' hospitals, doctors in certain circumstances and medical advice by radio. It requires shipowners to pay benefits to seafarers who have been injured or suffered illness on board. It also requires measures to protect the occupational safety and health of seafarers, including health promotion and accident prevention measures, shipboard programmes for risk avoidance and reduction, shipboard safety committees where there are five or more seafarers on board, and the duties of shipboard safety officers.

Title 4 also requires that shore-based welfare facilities for seafarers, where these are provided, are accessible and available to all seafarers irrespective of nationality, race, colour, sex, religion, political opinion or social origin. Finally, it sets out minimum requirements for social security protection for seafarers. It requires that at least three branches of social security be provided to all seafarers: medical care, sickness benefit and employment injury benefit.

Title 5: Compliance and enforcement

Title 5 sets out Flag State responsibilities for ensuring compliance with the Convention's requirements. All ships must carry a copy of the Convention on board.

Ships of 500 GT and over, that are not engaged exclusively on domestic voyages in the Flag State, must carry a Maritime Labour Certificate and a Declaration of Maritime Labour Compliance. The Maritime Labour Certificate will contain the name and details of the ship to which it applies and confirm that it has been inspected and found to be in compliance with the Flag State's laws implementing the Convention. It is valid for a maximum of 5 years. The working conditions that must be inspected and approved by a Flag State before it issues a Maritime Labour Certificate are:

'The Declaration of Maritime Labour Compliance shall be attached to the Maritime Labour Certificate. It shall have two parts; Part I, drawn up by the competent authority, sets out the Flag State requirements implementing the Convention, including any provisions that are substantially equivalent to provisions of Part A of the Code. Part II, drawn up by the shipowner, identifies the measures adopted to ensure ongoing compliance and continuous improvement. Flag State authorities are required to ensure that ships are inspected every five years, with intermediate inspections taking place between the second and third anniversary of the original inspection.'

Title 5 places a duty on the shipowner to draw up onboard complaint procedures for seafarers, to ensure that complaints concerning the non-provision of rights under the MLC are dealt with fairly and expeditiously.

It also sets out procedures for enforcement of the MLC by Port State Control authorities, including reporting requirements and powers in the event that deficiencies are identified. It describes the powers to detain ships where conditions on board are clearly hazardous to the safety, health or security of seafarers or where a non-conformity is identified that constitutes a serious or repeated breach of the requirements of the Convention. A ship's Maritime Labour Certificate and Declaration of Maritime Labour Compliance serve as evidence that the ship complies with the requirements of the MLC. Accordingly, the inspection by Port State Control officials is limited to a review of these documents unless there is other evidence justifying a more detailed inspection. Where a more detailed inspection identifies conditions that are clearly hazardous to the safety or health of seafarers, or there have been serious or repeated breaches of the MLC, detention of the ship is permitted for as long as is necessary for the rectification of the conditions or breaches.

Finally, Title 5 sets out the responsibilities of ratifying States with regard to seafarer recruitment and placement and the social protection of seafarers.

4.6 UK Employment Law for Seafarers

4.6.1 Registry of Shipping and Seamen

The Registry of Shipping and Seamen is the branch of the MCA that maintains the UK ship registry and issues Certificates of Competency (CoCs), Certificates of Equivalent Competency (CECs) identity documents and discharge books to seafarers. A seafarer's discharge book provides a record of employment. Ship operators are required to submit copies of their crew lists to the Registry, which enables it to maintain records of sea service. This is important for the qualification for and issuance of CoCs.

4.6.2 Work permits

Although there are, in principle, no nationality restrictions on employment on UK-registered ships (aside from the position of Master of a strategic ship), ships engaged in some trades are subject to similar requirements as shore-based businesses with regard to non-UK resident staff. Persons resident outside the EEA will require work permits to work on ships providing scheduled regular passenger or cargo services, as well as dredgers whose purpose is to ensure that approaches to ports are navigable. Granting a work permit will depend on the employer proving that no unemployed local resident is able to perform the vacant job and that the foreign candidate scores sufficiently highly in the Government's points-based system. In practice, the skill level required of any candidate currently exceeds the level required of a ship's Master, which means that, unless an annual salary in excess of £150,000 is offered, it will not be possible for a non-EEA resident to be employed on a vessel in such a trade.

4.6.3 Unfair dismissal and other statutory employment rights

A seafarer working on a ship registered in the UK will be entitled to claim a number of rights under the Employment Rights Act 1996 and other employment statutes, provided the vessel on which they are employed does not trade wholly outside the UK and they are ordinarily resident in the UK. Seafarers meeting these conditions may, therefore, benefit from numerous employment rights including the right to not be unfairly dismissed, to be paid at least the National Minimum Wage (NMW), to maternity and paternity leave and benefits, to time off for public and trade union duties and protection from detriment.

These rights may also apply to seafarers working on vessels registered outside the UK provided they can establish that the base of their employment is in the UK. This will depend on factors such as where the seafarer joins and leaves the ship, the currency in which they are paid and where they are liable for tax and social security payments.

4.6.4 Discipline, Code of Conduct, strikes and mutiny

Most UK shipping companies apply the Code of Conduct for the Merchant Navy to their crews. The Code of Conduct has been drawn up by the UK Chamber and the maritime unions Nautilus International and the National Union of Rail, Maritime and Transport Workers (RMT), and has been approved by the Maritime and Coastguard Agency (MCA) for application on merchant ships. It sets out standards of conduct expected in non-emergency situations and states that an emergency situation requires unquestioning obedience by all crew members of all orders. It also lists examples of gross misconduct, for which the appropriate sanction could be dismissal from the ship and from employment, and less serious misconduct, for which the highest sanction would be a final written warning. It also sets out a procedure to be followed on board and in shoreside offices in cases where there has been an alleged breach of the Code of Conduct.

Figure 4.10: The Code of Conduct, drawn up by the UK Chamber of Shipping

Strike action in a UK port will be subject to domestic UK laws governing strikes. A strike will be lawful if a registered UK trade union has secured a lawful majority in a secret ballot of the union members engaged in a trade dispute with their employer who would be called upon to take strike action. The union must also give notice (currently 7 days) to the employer of their intention to strike. In any other circumstances, the strike will not be lawful and the shipowner may seek a court injunction to prevent the strike and/or dismiss the striking seafarers.

Figure 4.11: Strike action in UK ports is subject to domestic legislation

Strike action while a vessel is at sea is expressly prohibited by Section 59 of the Merchant Shipping Act 1995 and is punishable by fines or imprisonment. Mutiny in modern times is an offence applicable to the armed forces, not to civilian seafarers.

4.7 UK Income Tax and National Insurance Regime for Seafarers

Seafarers resident in the UK are subject to UK income tax on their earnings. Overseas residents may also be liable to UK income tax if their work is performed wholly or mainly in the UK.

However, the UK Government applies a concession to seafarers exempting them from paying UK tax on their earnings as seafarers, provided they are physically outside the UK for 183 days in any tax year. This is called the Seafarers' Earning Deduction scheme (SED). Residents of other EEA Member States also benefit from this concession when working in the UK.

Liability of seafarers for UK National Insurance Contributions (NICs) will depend on where they are resident and where their ship is registered. Where their employer is based will determine whether or not NICs are due from the employer. However, the liability or otherwise of the employer will not affect the seafarer's entitlement to contributory benefits.

4.8   Health and Safety at Sea

UK-registered merchant ships are subject to the health and safety regime of the MCA, rather than the Health and Safety Executive (HSE), which regulates shore-based operations. Health and safety legislation for ships is mostly found in regulations made under Section 85 of the Merchant Shipping Act 1995, although some provisions have their origins in EU directives. UK health and safety laws may also be enforced on non-UK-registered ships when they are in UK territorial waters. Regulations are usually accompanied by Merchant Shipping Notices (MSNs) or Marine Guidance Notes (MGNs), which provide additional detail in easily comprehensible language. MSNs have quasi-statutory status: while MGNs are not mandatory, a company that has experienced an accident may need, in any resultant legal proceedings, to justify any decision not to comply with a relevant MGN.

Figure 4.12: Entry into an enclosed space is one of the more dangerous activities on board and strict guidance covers operations such as this

In addition to its role in making and enforcing health and safety laws, the MCA also publishes guidance to the industry on health and safety. The most significant of these is the Code of Safe Working Practices for Merchant Seafarers (COSWP), which has been drawn up in consultation with the UK Chamber of Shipping and the maritime trade unions in the UK. The COSWP includes sections providing general advice on living on board ship and managing shipboard health and safety, as well as detailed guidance relating to specific topics, including the use of personal protective equipment, manual handling of loads and protection from the adverse effects of noise and vibration. The MCA has also produced a series of posters and leaflets providing lifestyle advice to seafarers, covering topics such as sun-induced skin cancer and noise-induced hearing loss.

Code of Safe Working Practices for Merchant Seafarers

1. Managing Occupational Health and Safety
2. Safety Induction
3. Living On Board
4. Emergency Drills and Procedures
5. Fire Precautions
6. Security On Board
7. Health Surveillance
8. Personal Protective Equipment
9. Safety Signs and Their Use
10. Manual Handling
11. Safe Movement On Board Ship
12. Noise, Vibration and Other Physical Agents
13. Safety Officials
14. Permit to Work Systems
15. Entering Dangerous (Enclosed) Spaces
16. Hatch Covers and Access Lids
17. Work at Height
18. Provision, Care and Use of Work Equipment
19. Lifting Plant and Operations
20. Work on Machinery and Power Systems
21. Hazardous Substances and Mixtures
22. Boarding Arrangements
23. Food Preparation and Handling in the Catering Department
24. Hot Work
25. Painting
26. Anchoring, Mooring and Towing Operations
27. Roll-On/Roll-Off Ferries
28. Dry Cargo
29. Tankers and Other Ships Carrying Bulk Liquid Cargoes
30. Port Towage Industry
31. Ships Serving Offshore Oil and Gas Installations
32. Ships Serving Offshore Renewables Installations
33. Ergonomics

The UK Chamber and UK maritime trade unions have established a joint forum for the consideration of health and safety topics, called the National Maritime Occupational Health and Safety Committee (NMOHSC). This committee has developed guidelines to shipping companies on policies to combat alcohol misuse, drug abuse, HIV and AIDS and other infectious diseases, smoking, violence, aggression, verbal abuse and threats against staff on passenger ships and behavioural safety systems.

Key Point Summary

1) Subject to a small number of exceptions, the ship operator can choose any nationality of seafarer to work on their ships.

2) All seafarers must be trained and meet standards of competency set out in the STCW Convention.

3) The ship operator must ensure that all seafarers are provided with their entitlements under the Maritime Labour Convention, 2006 and may also need to take account of UK employment laws.

4) Seafarers may be exempted from paying income tax, while the ship operator may also be able to save costs by avoiding employers' National Insurance Contributions.

5) The ship operator has a duty to ensure that national and international health and safety rules applicable to ships are complied with.

Running a Shipping Business in the UK

5.1 Company Law Background

5.2 Taxation

5.3 Global Business and National Law

5.4 Employment of Seafarers

5.1   Company Law Background

Company law does not distinguish a shipping company from a company engaged in any other type of business and, although the term 'shipping company' is in general usage, there is no such thing in law as a shipping company. Any UK company that is properly incorporated and constituted may engage in the business of shipping.

The operation of ships, the carriage of goods, the carriage of passengers or the performance of maritime services offshore also do not require a licence. A company engaged in any such business must, of course, comply with all legal requirements relating to its ships and its corporate affairs, but it does not need a licence or any other kind of official authorisation. Shipping businesses in the UK operate in a genuinely free market.

One consequence of this situation, however, is that there is no reliable way of establishing how many UK shipping companies exist. There is no register of shipping companies and no way of identifying shipping companies within the register of companies at Companies House, nor is there a legal definition of what a 'shipping company' is.

5.2   Taxation

Figure 5.1: The Cunard Building in Liverpool, the former headquarters of the Cunard Line

5.2.1   Corporation Tax

All companies registered in the UK must register for Corporation Tax with HM Revenue and Customs. Tax law does not expressly recognise the concept of a shipping company, but it does contain special provisions relating to ships and to companies that own and operate them.

Corporation Tax is a tax on a company's profits. It is calculated as a rate (currently 19%) of taxable profits. Taxable profits are computed on a different basis to accounting profits and a company's taxable profit, therefore, usually differs from the profit stated in its published accounts.

Taxable profits, like accounting profits, represent the surplus of trading income over operating costs. However, they do not allow for depreciation, the concept where the capital cost of a business asset (such as a ship) is allocated across all the years in which it is used rather than shown as borne in full in the year in which it was actually bought. Capital expenditure is not deductible from trading income when calculating taxable profits.

Figure 5.2: The headquarters of HM Revenue & Customs in London. HMRC is the body responsible for Corporation Tax

Under the rules of Corporation Tax, a company is allowed to deduct a specified percentage of the cost of certain capital assets from its trading profits when calculating its taxable profits. This results in a lower taxable profit and, therefore, a smaller tax bill.

The rates of these 'capital allowances', and the type of assets in respect of which they can be claimed, are set out in law and change from time to time. They are fewer and less generous now than in the past, reflecting the progressive transformation of UK Corporation Tax since the 1980s from a regime with a high rate of tax alleviated by generous allowances to one with a low rate of tax and sparser allowances. In 1982, the rate of Corporation Tax stood at 52%, but UK shipowners could claim a capital allowance of 100% of the cost of a ship in the year they bought it (so that they could subtract the full cost of the ship from their taxable profit). Today, by contrast, while the rate of Corporation Tax is 19%, there are no special capital allowances that can be claimed in respect of ships.

Currently, the capital allowances available in respect of ships are the basic allowances for all 'plant and machinery'. These differ depending on whether or not the ship is deemed to be long-life asset (i.e. one with a useful economic life of at least 25 years when new). For a ship deemed to be a long-life asset, the company may claim a capital allowance of 8% per annum on a reducing balance basis (whereby 8% of its cost can be deducted from taxable profit in the first year, 8% of the remainder in the second year, and so on). For a ship deemed not to be a long-life asset, a capital allowance may be claimed at the rate of 18% per annum on a reducing balance basis.

One feature of the current capital allowance regime is unique to ships, conferring a specific benefit to companies that own them. A company that is eligible for a capital allowance in respect of a ship has the option to postpone all or part of that allowance to a subsequent tax period, enabling it to reduce its taxable profit when it is most beneficial. There would be little point, for example, in claiming the allowance in a year where the company made no profit at all.

A special capital allowance can be claimed on environmentally beneficial plant and machinery installed in ships. Where such plant and machinery is of a type specified by the Department of Energy and Climate Change (DECC) and meets certain energy saving criteria, the company may claim an allowance equal to its full value in the year it is bought.

Special arrangements also apply to the taxation of the proceeds from the sale of a ship. Where the proceeds from the sale of a typical capital asset exceed its written-down value (i.e. the purchase price, less the capital allowances that have been claimed in respect of it), the difference is taxable.

However, where the capital asset is a ship, the money can be held by the company for up to six years without attracting tax if it is subsequently re-invested in another ship. This 'roll-over relief' was introduced in 1995 (and then extended from three years to six in 1996), following a campaign by the UK Chamber that persuaded the Government that a company should be free to time its re-investments in new ships so as to take advantage of the cyclical fluctuations of the shipping market and not be penalised by a tax bill if a new ship was not bought in the same year as the old one was sold.

5.2.2   Tonnage tax

A company that operates ships may opt for its taxable profit to be determined solely by the tonnage of its fleet. Under this 'tonnage tax' arrangement, the company's daily profit per ship is calculated as follows:

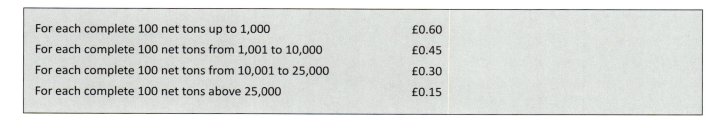

For each complete 100 net tons up to 1,000	£0.60
For each complete 100 net tons from 1,001 to 10,000	£0.45
For each complete 100 net tons from 10,001 to 25,000	£0.30
For each complete 100 net tons above 25,000	£0.15

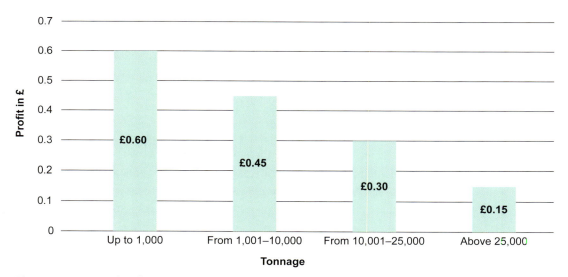

Figure 5.3: Example of a company's daily profits per ship in £ under the tonnage tax arrangement

That daily profit is multiplied by the number of days that the ship was operated by the company during the tax year in question. The resulting figure is the company's taxable profit for the year. Corporation Tax is then applied at the usual rate (of 19%) to this taxable profit in order to determine the amount of tax that is due.

Source: The economic impact of the UK Maritime Services Sector: Shipping (2015) – Oxford Economics.

UK Chamber of Shipping – Understanding UK Shipping

The amount of tax payable by a shipping company that has opted for tonnage tax is, therefore, not dependent on the actual profit made the company during the year. It is usually significantly less than would be payable if the company's taxable profits were calculated in the normal manner.

The purpose of the tonnage tax regime is to provide a low-tax environment that enables UK shipping companies to compete in world markets and attract overseas shipping companies to the UK. Its underlying objective is to stimulate economic activity and support skilled employment in the UK, thereby generating other tax revenues. Economic calculations show that, in 2013, £4.9bn of UK GDP was attributable to tonnage tax, 78,500 jobs were dependent on it and £1.2bn in tax revenue was generated by it.

Figure 5.4: Examples of ships eligible for tonnage tax

In order to be eligible for tonnage tax, a company must operate seagoing ships, of at least 100 GT, that are used for the carriage by sea of passengers or cargo, or for towage, salvage or other marine assistance carried out at sea, or for transport by sea in connection with other services of a kind necessarily provided at sea.

However, the following vessels types are not eligible:

* Fishing vessels or factory ships

* Pleasure craft (this does not mean cruise liners, which do qualify)

* Harbour or river ferries

* Offshore installations

* Tankers dedicated to a particular oil field

* Harbour tugs

* Harbour channel dredgers

* A vessel that has the main purpose of providing the goods or services normally provided on land (e.g. floating hotel or supermarket).

The company must also carry out the strategic and commercial management of its fleet in the UK. This test, which involves an assessment of how significant a part of the company's management is carried out in the UK rather than elsewhere, is intended to ensure that the company is engaged in significant economic activity in the UK and so contributes to the underlying objectives of the tonnage tax regime. Ordinarily, ships operated by UK tonnage tax companies are not subject to any flagging restrictions. However, eligible tugs and dredgers are required to be registered in an EU country and, in some years when the proportion of the overall tonnage tax fleet flying EU Flags has fallen, a tonnage tax company that acquires additional ships must register them in the EU.

A company that opts for tonnage tax is required to do so for all of its vessels and cannot claim any capital allowances on any ship it buys. The tonnage-based calculation replaces the normal profit-based calculation in respect of all its shipping income. Income from any non-shipping activities, however, is liable to Corporation Tax on the usual profit basis.

As a condition of opting for tonnage tax, a shipping company is required to invest in training new seafarers. Usually, it is required to train one officer cadet for every 15 officers it employs. With a cadetship taking three years, this equates to a requirement to take on one cadet every year for every five officers employed. If it suits the company to do so, it can opt to take on rating trainees instead of officer cadets, at a ratio of three rating trainees per cadet. The cadets or rating trainees must be British or EEA nationals and be ordinarily resident in the UK. Where a company is unable to fulfil its training requirement, perhaps because it has no berths for its full quota of cadets on board its ships, it is required to make an equivalent payment into a central maritime training fund.

Figure 5.5: A condition of the tax is investing in training new seafarers. Maritime colleges commonly use training simulators to familiarise cadets with elements of navigation, such as ECDIS

A shipping company that wishes to opt for tonnage tax must do so within six months of becoming eligible, i.e. within six months of both being subject to UK Corporation Tax and operating ships. This means that an existing UK company wishing to opt for tonnage tax must do so within six months of beginning to operate ships and a newly incorporated UK shipping company (whether it is an indigenous start-up or a foreign shipping company that has moved to the UK) must do so within six months of incorporation.

Having opted for tonnage tax, a company is then bound to have its taxable profit calculated on the basis of the tonnage of its fleet rather than the actual profitability of its business for the following ten years. It can renew its tonnage tax status annually. If it wishes to remain a tonnage tax company for the long term, it can always plan on a further ten years.

In 2015, there were 74 tonnage tax companies in the UK, operating a combined fleet of 760 ships. The fact that they have opted for tonnage tax is, like other aspects of their tax affairs, treated as confidential by HM Revenue and Customs. Their identity is therefore not known publicly unless the company concerned has chosen to declare its status as a tonnage tax company.

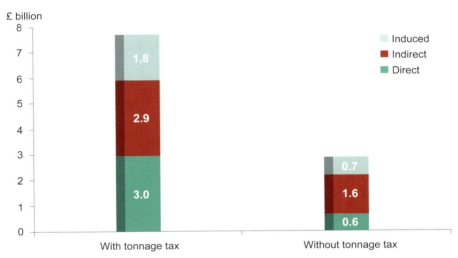

Source: UK Chamber of Shipping, Oxford Economics

Figure 5.6a: Estimated gross value added supported by the UK shipping industry, with and without tonnage tax in 2013

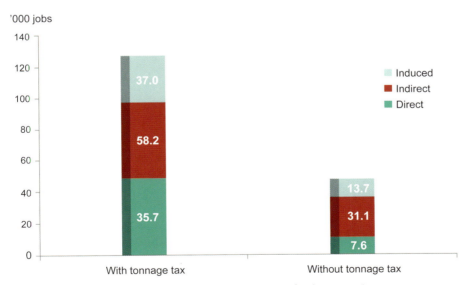

Source: UK Chamber of Shipping, Oxford Economics

Figure 5.6b: Estimated employment of UK nationals in the shipping industry, with and without tonnage tax in 2013

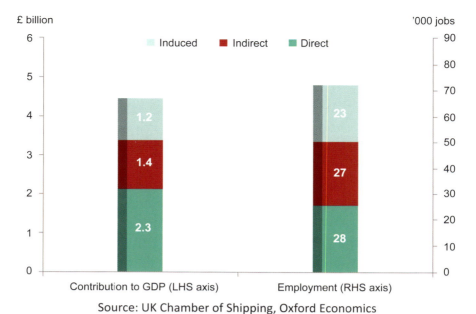

Source: UK Chamber of Shipping, Oxford Economics

Figure 5.6c: The total benefits of tonnage tax as compared to counterfactual scenario without tonnage tax in 2013

5.2.3   EU State aid framework

State aid, which includes preferential tax regimes whereby certain companies pay less tax than usual as well as straightforward cash handouts from Governments to favoured businesses, is generally prohibited by EU law. However, it may be permitted on an exceptional basis if it is deemed to be justified. Shipping is a sector where State aid is deemed to be justifiable, because of its importance to the EU economy and the difficulties that European shipping companies face in competing in a free global market with overseas shipping companies that have a lower cost base.

All special tax regimes for shipping companies in the UK are subject to approval by the European Commission. Approval is dependent on compatibility with the Commission's Guidelines on State Aid to Maritime Transport, as last updated in 2004.

The Guidelines set out the types of State aid regimes that are permitted and stipulate the general EU objectives to which such regimes must contribute. These objectives are:

The types of State aid regimes that may be permitted if they contribute towards these objectives are identified by the Guidelines as:

- Preferential corporate tax arrangements for shipping companies (such as tonnage tax, special capital allowances for ships and roll-over relief)

- Reduced rates of personal income tax and national insurance for seafarers

- Government subsidies for the training of seafarers

- Start-up grants for short sea shipping services

- Operating subsidies for lifeline ferry services.

There is no requirement for EU Member States to introduce any such regime, but any EU Member State that wishes to do so (or to amend an existing regime) must apply to the European Commission for approval, demonstrating that the regime is compatible with the Guidelines. Where State aid is granted without such approval, the Commission can require the Government of the Member State concerned to reclaim the aid from the beneficiary.

The special tax arrangements for shipping companies in the UK (outlined in Sections 5.2.1 and 5.2.2) have all been approved in this way. Similar arrangements, likewise approved under the Commission's Guidelines, exist in other Member States. For example, all maritime Member States have a tonnage tax regime.

5.3   Global Business and National Law

Most areas of law, apart from tax, neither acknowledge that UK shipping companies operate in a global business environment nor make any special provision for them. The conflict between a national legal framework that reflects domestic political priorities and the reality of having to operate in a global market where customers, suppliers and competitors are not bound by UK standards is most obvious in relation to immigration and business ethics.

5.3.1 Visas

The UK shipping sector, like its counterparts elsewhere in the EU, is reliant on recruiting personnel from around the world in order to make up the shortfall of suitably qualified and experienced UK/EEA nationals. Domestic political considerations in the UK have made it increasingly difficult in recent years to bring in expertise from overseas, whether that is by recruiting new employees under the Tier 2 general visas regime or by transferring existing personnel from their overseas branches under the Tier 2 intra-company transfer (ICT) visa route.

5.3.2 Business ethics

As a jurisdiction and a place to do business, the UK has a justified reputation for probity and, since the introduction of the Bribery Act 2010, the UK has had one of the strictest statutory anti-corruption regimes in the world. Unlike comparable regimes elsewhere, it is extra-territorial in scope (so that it holds UK companies liable for the actions of their personnel and their agents overseas as well as in the UK) and it fails to acknowledge a distinction between bribery (paying money to secure something to which the company has no legal entitlement) and facilitation payments (paying money to an individual who otherwise refuses to provide the service or perform a task for which the company has already paid).

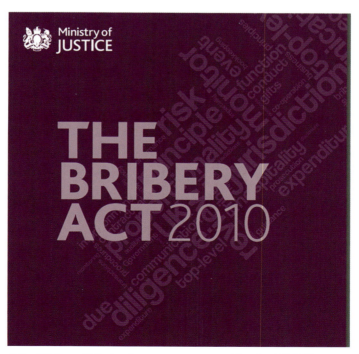

Figure 5.7: Ethics within business are governed by the UK Bribery Act 2010

Some countries either permit overseas facilitation payments that are low level, routine and are required, despite the payer already being entitled to the service or goods in question (and therefore the payer is effectively being extorted), or identify them as grounds on which a company should not be prosecuted. The UK's prohibition on such payments runs counter to the expectations of those working in ports in many parts of the world, where facilitation payments (whether they be food stuffs, cigarettes, alcohol or small cash payments) may be regarded as normal supplements to their salaries.

5.3.3   Sanctions

Trade and financial sanctions serve as a non-military means of restricting the activities of foreign Governments (or individuals) that are deemed to pose a threat. The UK, as a trading country with an active foreign policy, maintains and enforces a complex regime of sanctions, implementing United Nations and EU restrictions and targeting other individuals who are deemed to pose a particular threat to the UK. In broad terms, the regime is twofold: restrictions on the export of certain things and restrictions on financial dealings. Both types of sanctions affect shipping companies.

Trade sanctions typically cover items such as military weapons, chemical precursors and equipment that can be used for internal repression, although, in recent years, particular sanctions regimes have targeted the Iranian oil industry and the Libyan aviation sector with restrictions on harmless engineering technology. These restrictions are mostly enforced as part of the usual Customs regime of export controls (which also covers endangered animal species and works of art), so that the compliance burden falls on the exporter rather than the shipping company. Shipping companies do, however, come within the scope if they trans-ship at a UK port goods to which sanctions apply. UK shipping companies are prohibited from carrying such goods, regardless of where they originate.

Financial sanctions typically prohibit the payment of money, the provision of loans or other financial services (including insurance) or the provision of brokering facilities to designated individuals and entities, such as terrorist groups and their associates. These sanctions must be observed by all companies operating from the UK and they can create significant, and sometimes insuperable, compliance difficulties in countries where port agents are State-owned monopolies and connected to designated individuals in the Government.

5.4   Employment of Seafarers

UK companies are required to pay employers' National Insurance Contributions (NICs) in respect of their employees. The National Insurance scheme is universal, unlike equivalent schemes in other EU countries that provide exemptions (in a variety of forms) for seafarers.

UK shipping companies can, however, avoid liability for employers' NICs by entering into arrangements with offshore companies for the employment of their crews. Practically all UK-based commercial shipping companies source their crews from companies or agencies whose headquarters are in Guernsey, Bermuda or Singapore, since employers based outside of the EEA are not liable for employers' NICs. (The seafarers themselves *are* required to pay contributions.) To benefit from this, the overseas-based employer must be able to demonstrate that it is genuinely the employer of the seafarers, taking responsibility for matters such as paying wages, issuing seafarer employment agreements and disciplinary procedures.

Companies operating ships that operate wholly within UK waters (Categories A–D) are not able to avoid employers' NICs in respect of the crews of those ships as they are subject to domestic laws with regard to contribution liability.

Key Point Summary

1) Company law does not distinguish a shipping company from a company engaged in any other type of business.

2) Special provisions exist within the framework of Corporation Tax for ships and for companies that operate ships. Ships, like other plant and machinery, qualify for capital allowances. Uniquely, proceeds from ship sales can be kept for up to six years tax-free for re-investment in further tonnage. Companies that operate ships can opt to have their taxable profit calculated on the basis of the tonnage of their fleet rather than the actual profitability of their business, known as 'tonnage tax'.

3) Special tax arrangements must comply with EU State aid rules. Preferential tax breaks are usually prohibited but may be permitted for shipping companies, subject to certain conditions, to enable European businesses to compete in world markets.

4) UK shipping companies sometimes get caught in a conflict between global business and domestic law, which imposes UK business ethics on their operations in very different parts of the world and prevents UK companies from having commercial dealings with certain overseas countries or entities that are subject to sanctions.

5) Unlike other EU countries, the UK makes no special provisions for seafarers in its National Insurance scheme. As a result, most seafarers working on ships operated by UK companies are contracted by employers based outside the EU, where they are outside the scope of the scheme.

The UK Shipping Market

6.1   The Open Coast Policy

The UK operates an 'open coast' policy, which means that all ships are permitted to call at UK ports and to compete for business, whether carrying cargo or passengers, laying or maintaining pipelines and cables, servicing offshore installations or performing any other tasks for reward at sea. Ships are required to meet all international regulatory standards (such as those relating to safety and the environment), but there are no restrictions based on the Flag they fly or on the nationality of their owners.

Figure 6.1:   The UK has historically always been a seafaring nation with an established merchant navy

This policy has been in place since 1849, when the Navigation Acts of the 17th century were repealed. The Navigation Acts had reserved British trade for British ships, forbidding foreign ships from carrying cargo between Britain and its colonies. They embodied the prevailing political view that Britain's international trade 'belonged' to Britain and that paying foreign ships to carry this trade would represent an unthinkable loss of national wealth. Enacted to increase shipping and encourage navigation, the Navigation Acts are remembered principally as a contributory cause of war with Holland (as their main effect was to exclude Dutch ships from British trade) and for stoking resentment in the American colonies (due to the obligation to sell their produce through British merchants only).

The repeal of the Navigation Acts in the middle of the 19th century, alongside the abolition of the Corn Laws (which had imposed prohibitively high taxes on imported grain), represented a complete rejection of protectionist trade policies. A new political and economic consensus had taken hold, that the national interest was best served by free trade; open markets would give consumers in Britain access to goods at the lowest price, stimulating economic activity and the creation of wealth. This belief in free trade and open markets has guided UK shipping policy ever since.

The significance of the UK's open coast policy becomes clear when it is compared with the regulation of shipping markets in other countries.

6.2   The International Context

6.2.1   International shipping markets

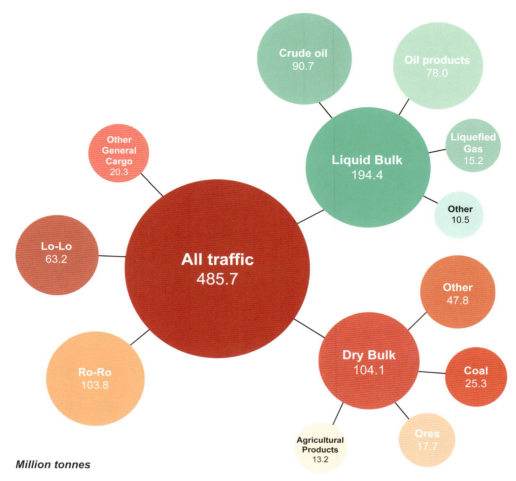

Million tonnes

Source: Department for Transport, UK Port Freight Statistics, 2015
Figure 6.2a: UK major port traffic by cargo type, 2015

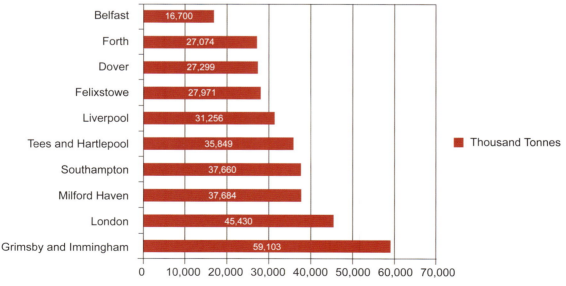

Source: Department for Transport, UK Port Freight Statistics, 2015
Figure 6.2b: Top ten busiest UK ports in terms of total tonnage

The UK's policy of allowing all ships, regardless of nationality or ownership, to carry its international trade is mirrored by the majority of developed countries with democratic governments. It was taken up by the European Economic Community in 1986 and the principle of maintaining a regime of fair and free competition in international shipping markets is now guaranteed in European law. There is an open market in the carriage of passengers or goods by sea between any port in an EU country and any port or offshore installation (such as an oil rig) in another EU country.

Similarly, in 1987, the Organisation for Economic Co-operation and Development (OECD) committed itself to the principle of:

... free circulation of shipping in international trade in free and fair competition as a guarantee of adequate and economic world shipping services and of maximum economic benefit for shipowners, shippers and consumers.

All countries that are members of the OECD (currently there are 34) are required, as a condition of membership, to maintain an open market in their international shipping trades.

By contrast, a number of countries (mostly in the developing world, but including some wealthy 'command economies') restrict access to their international shipping markets. Access is usually controlled through a licensing regime, where shipowners need a licence to load or discharge cargo at the country's ports and such licences are granted only to that country's 'own' shipowners and to favoured foreigners. Typically, foreign shipowners are granted licences on the basis of reciprocity between the countries concerned or on the basis of the infamous cargo sharing formula in the UNCTAD Code of Conduct for Liner Conferences.

Adopted in 1973, the UNCTAD Code reflected the desire of many newly independent countries to develop their own merchant fleets, as engines of economic growth and symbols of national pride. It reserved the right to carry at least 80% of the trade between any two countries to shipowners of those two countries, with each entitled to an equal share. The residue, up to 20% of the total, was then available to shipowners from other countries.

The Code did not (and could not) create national merchant fleets in the countries that signed up to it. All it created was a legal right to carry cargo. In order to administer these rights, licensing regimes were created and, where no indigenous shipowners existed, their licences were sold to foreign shipowners who were otherwise excluded from the country's trade. The country derived an income, but the licence cost was necessarily built into the freight rates charged by the shipowner, so that it was borne ultimately by the country's own exporters and its consumers.

6.2.2   Domestic trades (cabotage)

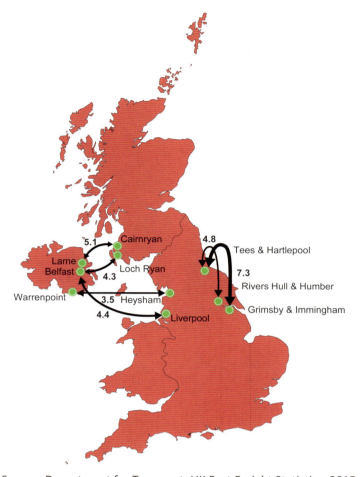

Source: Department for Transport, UK Port Freight Statistics, 2015
Figure 6.3: Top UK domestic routes (million tonnes), 2015

The UK's open coast policy encompasses all ships on all voyages. Many other countries, including several in the EU, regulate access to their domestic shipping market differently from their international trades. EU law similarly distinguishes between international and domestic trades.

Partly as a consequence of the geography of the British Isles and the wealth of its offshore resources, the UK has a vibrant and multi-faceted domestic shipping market. Ferries sail between Great Britain and Northern Ireland and between the British mainland and the Isle of Wight and the Scottish islands. Regular services by feeder container vessels and shuttle tankers link UK ports. Bulk ships carry grain and fertiliser around the coast and bring stone from Scottish quarries, while dredgers bring sand and gravel ashore for use in construction. Vessels of various types service the offshore oil rigs in the North Sea. In 2014, UK domestic shipping traffic exceeded 25bn tonne-kilometres and no restrictions, beyond compliance with international regulatory standards, apply to ships in these trades.

By contrast, thirteen EU Member States (more than half of those with a coastline) restrict access to their domestic shipping trades on the basis of the Flag flown by the ship: Bulgaria, Croatia, Estonia, Finland, France, Germany, Greece, Italy, Lithuania, Portugal, Slovenia, Spain and Sweden. EU law prohibits any discrimination between ships registered in EU Member States, and requires those Member States that control their domestic shipping trades to grant access to ships registered in any EU Member State. Ships registered outside the EU need a licence to carry passengers or cargo on domestic voyages in those thirteen Member States, and such licences will usually be granted only in circumstances where no suitable EU-flagged vessel is available.

Similar restrictive regimes exist in other countries, including the USA. Under the terms of the Jones Act, a ship must be built in the US, flagged in the US and manned by US personnel in order to be entitled to operate in the US domestic shipping markets.

Compliance with these stipulations is expensive as the price of a container vessel built in a US shipyard is approximately five times greater than one built in Korea and US domestic shipping services consequently have a very high cost base. The shipment of containers between the US mainland and its islands (Hawaii and Puerto Rico) is estimated to cost over $1bn annually more than it would if those trades were open to global competition and there is virtually no shipping of containers between ports on the coast of the US mainland because carriage by road and rail is cheaper.

Figure 6.4: **The US has a restrictive regime that requires certain trade to be carried out by US shipping. Compliance with these requirements is enforced by US Customs and Coastguard Authorities**

Japan, China, Brazil and Australia, among many other countries, also reserve the right to carry cargo between their ports to ships flying their own Flags.

It is worth noting that restrictions on access to domestic shipping markets are generally based on where ships are registered, which contrasts with the much rarer restrictions on access to international markets that are usually based on the nationality of the shipowner.

6.3   Work Permits for Seafarers Working in UK Trades

The majority of ships trading into and out of UK ports are crewed with seafarers from all over the world. This is the case even with most ships operated by UK companies. There are very few provisions restricting employment on UK ships to particular nationals.

However, the position is different for ships that operate on some UK-only routes. The UK imposes restrictions on foreign nationals seeking to take any employment in the UK, through the application of a points-based system that determines whether a vacancy should be offered to a foreign national. No restrictions apply to workers who are nationals of Member States of the EEA, who enjoy free movement throughout the EEA, but other nationals need to satisfy the test applied by the points-based system, which relates to their qualifications for the job vacancy they wish to take. The potential employer must also demonstrate that there is no locally-based unemployed person capable of performing the job.

The points-based system applies to the following shipping trades:			
Ships that operate wholly within UK waters (Categories A–D)	Scheduled passenger and cargo services operating in accordance with a published timetable between the same two or more ports	Inshore dredging vessels	Vessels whose function is limited to the servicing of wind farms located within UK territorial waters

Any seafarer would need to enter the UK under Tier 2 of the points-based system, which applies to skilled workers who have been offered employment in the UK. In practice, no seafarer from outside the EEA would be accepted for employment on a ship in these trades, since the minimum qualification requirement is far above the level of even a ship Master's Certificate of Competency.

Ships not falling into these categories are free to employ whichever nationalities of seafarers they choose, as the points-based system will not apply.

Further details on the crewing of ships can be found in Chapter 4 – Crewing and Employment.

6.4   The Open Port Duty

The open coast policy is buttressed by a duty on operators of UK ports to admit all persons that wish to use them for loading and discharging a ship. All shipowners, therefore, have a legal right not only to compete for business carrying goods or passengers to, from or within the UK, but also to use any UK port in order to perform this business. Like the open coast policy, this open port duty dates from the middle of the 19th century.

Figure 6.5: Aberdeen Harbour, Scotland

As a matter of European law, this general prohibition on port operators discriminating between ships has been extended specifically to port charges. Port dues that vary according to the Flag of a ship or according to where it has arrived from or is sailing to are prohibited. A port operator is permitted to impose differential charges on ships only to the extent that the difference reflects the objective cost of providing services to the ship.

Key Point Summary

1)   In the UK, as in the rest of the EU and in all developed countries, all shipowners are free to compete for business carrying goods and passengers on international voyages.

2)   Similarly, all shipowners are free to compete for business in the UK's domestic shipping trades, with ships under any Flag.

3)   On certain domestic trades, work permit rules restrict employment to nationals of the UK and other EEA Member States.

4)   The open coast policy is supported by a requirement on UK ports to allow any shipowner to use their facilities on payment of dues, which must not discriminate on the basis of nationality.

Trading and Operating a Ship

7.1   General

This chapter begins by looking at the support that a company involved in the operation of ships on scheduled or regular services on fixed routes must provide. Fixed routes are generally ferry routes operating between two ports, but often with additional calls to a third or other port as a part of their schedule. Liner and tramp shipping services are not subject to these measures. A number of regulatory requirements address the need for an additional measure of oversight of ships engaged in such regular services, particularly as many fixed routes carry high numbers of passengers. Regional oversight of such routes is especially difficult on intra-EU passenger carrying services and additional requirements are contained in *Council Directive 1999/35/EC on a system of mandatory surveys for the safe operation of regular Ro-Ro ferry and high-speed passenger craft services*.

All ships must comply with marine regulatory requirements when operating. Although these do vary with ship type, and in accordance with their Class, in the UK all ships (including cargo and passenger ships) over 500 GT must comply with the ISM and ISPS Codes. These govern the safety management systems (SMSs) and security procedures that a company must ensure are practised on its vessels during all operations at sea and in port.

Figure 7.1: Member States of the EU

7.1.1 Application

Council Directive 1999/35/EC applies to all RoRo ferries and high speed passenger craft operating a regular service, domestically or internationally, to or from a port of a Member State, regardless of their Flag. Its purpose is to:

- Define a system of mandatory surveys capable of better ensuring the safe operation of regular RoRo ferry and high-speed passenger craft services to or from ports in EU States

- Provide the right for the Member State (of the port) to conduct, participate in or cooperate with any investigation of maritime casualties on these services.

The Directive provides that, prior to the start of operation of a regular RoRo ferry or high-speed passenger craft service, the State must check that:

- Companies operating or intending to operate such ferries or craft:

  » Take the measures necessary for the application of the specific requirements (right of the Master to take the necessary decisions, log of navigational activities and incidents, reporting of damage to shell doors, providing persons on board the craft with general information to assist them)

  » Agree in advance that the host State or any other Member State particularly concerned may carry out, participate fully in or cooperate in any investigation of a marine casualty or incident and provide them with access to the information retrieved from the voyage data recorder (VDR) of any of their vessels involved in a casualty

- For vessels flying a Flag other than that of a Member State, the administration of that Flag State has accepted the company's commitment to fulfil the requirements of the Directive

- RoRo ferries and high speed passenger craft meet the following requirements:

  » Hold valid certificates issued by the administration of the Flag State, which means they must be surveyed for the issue of certificates in accordance with IMO regulations

> » Comply with the Classification standards specified for the construction and maintenance of their hull, machinery and electrical and control installation
>
> » Be fitted with a voyage data recorder (VDR) for the purpose of providing information on any casualty occurring
>
> » Comply with the specific stability requirements adopted at regional level, provided that those requirements do not go beyond those specified in the Annex to Resolution 14 of the 1995 SOLAS Conference.

The Directive states that each host State must carry out an initial specific survey to ensure that the RoRo ferry or high-speed passenger craft fulfils all the conditions to operate a safe regular service to or from one or more of its ports.

This survey must be carried out before the ship begins the regular service, be reviewed annually and be subject to exceptional inspections if material changes to the ship or route are made.

> The Directive makes provision for substantially interested Member States to take part in any investigation concerning maritime casualties involving a RoRo ferry or a high-speed passenger craft operating a regular service to or from a Community port. It also makes provision for several accompanying measures, including the following:
>
> - Collaboration between the host State and the administration of the Flag State concerned regarding the suitability of exemptions
>
> - Establishment of shore-based navigational guidance systems
>
> - Communication to the Commission of a copy of the survey reports
>
> - Ability to implement an integrated system of contingency planning for shipboard emergencies
>
> - Establishment of operating restrictions.

The Commission maintains a database of the inspection reports provided by Member States and will inform third party countries, who bear either Flag State or host State responsibilities, of the requirements imposed on any company providing a regular service to or from a Community port.

These are additional requirements and a vessel is also required to be certified in accordance with the requirements of its Class (see Chapter 3).

7.2   Shipboard and Company Procedures – ISM Code

Figure 7.2: The ISM Code

7.2.1   Statutory requirements for operating a ship

The ISM Code establishes an international standard for the safe management and operation of ships by setting rules for the organisation of company management in relation to safety and pollution prevention and for the implementation of a safety management system (SMS).

7.2.2   Application

> The provisions of Chapter IX of the SOLAS Convention and the ISM Code apply to:
>
> - International registered ships of 500 GT and above, engaged on international voyages and propelled by mechanical means and the Companies that they belong to
>
> - Passenger ships engaged on international voyages and the Companies that they belong to.

'Company' means the owner of the ship or any other organisation or person, such as the manager or the bareboat charterer, who has assumed the responsibility for operation of the ship from the shipowner and who, on assuming such responsibility, has agreed to take over all duties and responsibility imposed by the ISM Code.

7.2.3   Objectives

The objectives of the ISM Code are to ensure safety at sea, prevent human injury or loss of life and avoid damage to the environment and property.

> The ISM Code establishes the following three overarching safety management objectives:
>
> - Provide safe practices in ship operation and working environment
>
> - Establish safeguards against all identified risks
>
> - Continuously improve safety management skills of personnel ashore and on board ships; these skills include preparation for safety and environmental emergencies.

7.2.4   Requirements

The ISM Code requires every company to develop, implement and maintain a safety management system (SMS) that includes the following functional requirements:

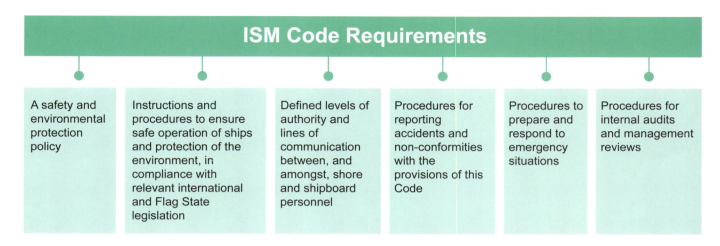

ISM Code Requirements
A safety and environmental protection policy	Instructions and procedures to ensure safe operation of ships and protection of the environment, in compliance with relevant international and Flag State legislation	Defined levels of authority and lines of communication between, and amongst, shore and shipboard personnel	Procedures for reporting accidents and non-conformities with the provisions of this Code	Procedures to prepare and respond to emergency situations	Procedures for internal audits and management reviews

7.2.5   Documents and certificates

Figure 7.3:   An example of ship certificates on board

A company that operates a ship to which the ISM Code applies needs to have a Document of Compliance (DOC) or an Interim DOC. A company will receive a DOC or Interim DOC after it has been verified that it complies with the relevant requirements of the ISM Code. An up-to-date copy of the DOC should be placed on board ships operated by the company.

A ship to which the ISM Code applies will receive a Safety Management Certificate (SMC) or Interim SMC after it has been verified that its shipboard management and its company operate in accordance with the approved SMS.

ISM certificates are valid for a period of 5 years, subject to an intermediate verification.

7.3   Shipboard and Port Facility Security Procedures – ISPS Code

7.3.1   Background

Figure 7.4: The ISPS Code

Following the terrorism events of September 2001, the International Maritime Organization (IMO) agreed to develop security measures applicable to ships and port facilities. These security measures have been included as amendments to the Safety of Life at Sea Convention, 1974 (SOLAS Convention) in Chapter XI-2. Part A of the Code is mandatory and Part B is recommendatory.

The security measures were accepted internationally on 1st January 2004 and came into force six months later on 1st July 2004.

7.3.2   International Ship and Port Facility Security Code (ISPS Code)

The IMO security regime in Chapter XI-2 is designed to be preventive in nature and it applies to both ships and the port facilities that ships use. Ships subject to the Code are passenger ships and high-speed passenger craft, cargo ships and high-speed craft of 500 GT and upwards and mobile offshore drilling units. Ports to which it applies are those serving international voyages.

At a regional level, EU Directive 725/2004, on enhancing ship and port facility security, implements the ISPS Code in Member States and extends certain provisions to passenger ships on domestic services. Following a risk assessment, the regulation was further extended to additional domestic ships on a national basis. The Ship and Port Facility (Security) Regulations 2004 enacted UK measures.

The objectives of the ISPS Code are to:

- Establish an international framework involving cooperation between contracting governments, government agencies, local administrations and the shipping and port industries to detect/assess security threats and take preventive measures against security incidents affecting ships or port facilities used in international trade

- Establish the respective roles and responsibilities of all these parties concerned, at the national and international level, for ensuring maritime security

- Ensure the early and efficient collation and exchange of security-related information

- Provide a methodology for security assessments so as to have in place plans and procedures to react to changing security levels

- Ensure confidence that adequate and proportionate maritime security measures are in place.

The objectives are to be achieved through the designation of appropriate security officers/personnel on each ship, in each port facility and in each shipping company, to prepare and to put into effect the security plans that will be approved for each ship and port facility.

7.3.3 Key elements of the ISPS Code

The Code allows security measures to be adjusted to meet the specific risks facing particular ships or port facilities:

- **Part A** contains mandatory provisions covering the appointment of security officers for shipping companies, individual ships and port facilities

- **Part B** contains guidance and recommendations on preparing ship and port facility security plans.

In the UK, the Maritime Transport Security and Resilience Division of the Department for Transport are responsible for overseeing ISPC Code requirements. They publish guidance for companies producing security plans for different ship types, and for ports. Certification requirements are aligned with those of the ISM Code and issued by the Maritime and Coastguard Agency.

The ISPS Code contains the following three security levels that are set by government:

Figure 7.5: ISPS security levels with an example of a security level notice on board

Security Level 3 will imply that a port facility and ships at that facility will rely on instructions, in the case of UK ports from the Department for Transport, and follow them as required. Security Level 3 is likely to involve other governmental responses.

7.4 Carriage of Goods by Sea

As a general principle, shipping companies (as carriers) and their customers (as shippers or charterers) are free to agree price and other contractual conditions by mutual agreement. To facilitate transactions, and to harmonise requirements and liabilities, standard documents have been developed. Bills of Lading (B/Ls) or Waybills are in day-to-day use and allow the relevant international conventions, such as the Hague-Visby Rules, to be observed or implemented.

A complex international regime comprising the Hague Rules, the Hague-Visby Rules, the Hamburg Rules and the Rotterdam Rules governs international practices of carriage. The rules are required for many different cargo types and different voyages, where handling and stowage practices may vary widely. In UK law, the Carriage of Goods by Sea Act 1971 implemented the Hague-Visby Rules, and the Carriage of Goods by Sea Act 1992 further extended the law's coverage to permit the use of modern electronic alternative transport documents.

The law is concerned with the rights of the person buying goods that are to be transported by sea and the liabilities of the carrier and it provides protection against goods in transit being lost or damaged.

The Act obliges the carrier to issue a B/L to the shipper whenever one is demanded by the shipper. The functions of the B/L are:

- To serve as a receipt for goods received

- To act as evidence of the contract of carriage

- To serve as a Document of Title, which facilitates the sale or trading of goods in transit.

While a Bill of Lading is usually a transferable Document of Title (the lawful holder of the Bill of Lading is automatically the owner of the goods), a Sea Waybill, by contrast, is not a document of title and the holder of a Waybill has no conferred ownership. The handling of such a document is therefore more straightforward and Waybills can be transmitted electronically because no harm is caused if someone other than the lawful owner of the goods receives and prints a copy. Bills of Lading cannot be transmitted electronically.

7.4.1   The role of the Master

The Master is the shipowner's representative on board but is also under a duty to carry out the charterer's instructions where the vessel is on a time or voyage charter. The Master is the agent for the carrier in a contract for the carriage of goods by sea. When cargo is loaded, the Master, or more usually the ship's agent on behalf of the Master, will issue a Mate's Receipt to the shipper. This will indicate that the cargo has been loaded and whether the cargo is damaged – in which case the agent will issue a Claused Bill of Lading stating so. If the cargo is in good condition, a Clean Bill of Lading will be issued. Once the cargo is delivered to the receiver or Consignee, the Master or his agent will mark it as Accomplished. At sea, the Master is responsible for properly stowing the cargo and providing a seaworthy ship.

Figure 7.6: A ship's Master

7.4.2   Ship procedures and practices

When operating a vessel, a ship's crew, under the authority of the Master, should follow established maritime traditions and practices, in accordance with the regulatory requirements of the Flag State and international law. Such practices will involve the safe voyage of the vessel, the safe unloading and loading of cargo and the prevention of pollution at sea.

The Safety Management System (SMS), a requirement of the ISM Code, provides the ship's crew with checklists and procedures to carry out these operations safely. Records are maintained at sea and in port by officers on board to ensure a narrative of events is kept for reference and that tasks are being carried out safely. Log books are filled out by the ship's officers and Master. Records kept on board British ships include, among others:

- The Official Log Book – entries are made to record such activities as births, deaths, accidents, drills, training, testing, inspections, maintenance, departures and arrivals

- The Deck Log Book – this records navigational activities to show a complete record of the ship's voyage from port to port

- The Cargo Log Book – this records loading, carriage and unloading of the ship's cargo

- The GMDSS Radio Log – this is the ship's radio log showing all radio communications carried out utilising the shipboard Global Maritime Distress and Safety System

- The Oil Record Book – all ships over 400 GT will keep a record book of machinery space operations and all tankers over 150 GT must keep a record of cargo and ballast operations.

Figure 7.7: Records must be kept on board to show compliance with the ISM Code

Key Point Summary

1) Passenger ships on regular routes are subject to more exhaustive regulatory oversight due to the large numbers of passengers they carry.

2) The safety management of ships, including both company and shipboard procedures, is contained in the International Safety Management (ISM) Code, which requires the issuance of a Document of Compliance to the shore office and a Safety Management Certificate (SMC) to the ship.

3) The security management of ships and ports is controlled by the International Ship and Port Facility (ISPS) Code and European regulation.

4) A complex international regime of contract law covers the carriage of goods by sea. In UK law, the Carriage of Goods by Sea Act 1971 details national provisions.

Ports and their Customers

8.1   Introduction

In terms of tonnage handled, the UK ports sector is the largest in Europe. It is comprised of a number of ownership models with company, trust and municipal ports all operating commercially, independently of government and very largely without public subsidy. The private sector operates 15 of the largest 20 ports by tonnage and around two-thirds of the UK's port traffic. Much of the tonnage handled is concentrated in a small number of ports, with the top 15 ports accounting for more than 80% of the UK's total traffic. There is no standard governance model, but UK ports generally operate efficiently in serving the demands of their users.

Ports in the UK are owned and operated by three types of authority. Historically, private ports and company-owned ports were developed to serve a particular commercial activity, for example to provide an oil terminal; Felixstowe was an exception and was developed as a general facility. In the 1990s, seven former trust ports were privatised. About 70% of UK ports are privatised. Internationally, this is unusual; the majority EU model is for ports to be in public ownership and this has in the past raised competition issues.

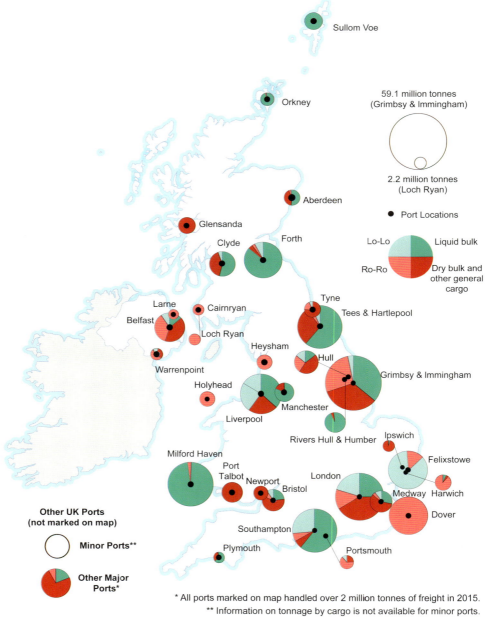

* All ports marked on map handled over 2 million tonnes of freight in 2015.
** Information on tonnage by cargo is not available for minor ports.

Source: Department for Transport, UK Port Freight Statistics, 2015

Figure 8.1: UK ports and tonnage figures

Ports that are not privately owned are public trust ports or trust ports established by individual Acts of Parliament and are controlled by independent statutory bodies, often known as Conservancy Boards or Harbour Commissioners. A number of other ports are controlled by municipal authorities, where the local authority acts as landlord. Municipal ports are usually small, with the exceptions being Sullom Voe and Portsmouth.

The Government's policy is to continue with a mixed ownership model, although it is aware of the potential competitive disadvantage this may cause in relation to publicly funded EU ports. As in other areas of EU regulation, a perception exists that UK ports suffer from overregulation, especially in relation to the environment, which may hinder the commercial development of adequate and timely new port infrastructure.

8.2　Harbour Regulation

8.2.1　Harbour authorities

Harbour authorities ensure the safe and efficient operation of harbours, taking responsibility for ships and persons within the harbour, navigation and the safety of the port environment. Competent harbour authorities also have a duty to consider what pilotage services, if any, need to be provided.

A competent harbour authority is defined in the Pilotage Act 1987 and means any harbour authority:

- That has statutory powers in relation to the regulation of shipping movements and the safety of navigation within its harbour, and

- Whose harbour falls wholly or partly within an active former pilotage district.

8.2.2 Port Marine Safety Code

The Port Marine Safety Code (PMSC), 2000, developed a national standard for port marine safety in the UK, aiming to improve safety standards for vessels, passengers, cargo and crew. To comply with the Code, harbour authorities should frequently review both their risk assessment and safety management systems and their existing powers under local and national legislation, making adjustments and revisions where necessary.

8.2.3 Harbour and other directions

The Marine Navigation Act 2013 gives harbour authorities the power to make harbour directions, which are instructions designed to better regulate shipping and to improve safety within the harbour area.

Harbour directions are used to regulate ships entering, leaving or within a harbour and may relate to:

- The movement of ships (i.e. to regulate the use of any main navigation channel or fairway)

- The mooring and unmooring of ships (where and how vessels may moor)

- Ship's equipment (for example, the provision of enough radios to allow communication between the harbour and the vessel)

- Ship's machinery

- The manning of ships.

Harbour directions will only apply to ships as defined in the Harbours Act 1964, which defines a ship as including every description of vessel used in navigation, seaplanes and hovercraft.

The UK Government outlines four powers available to harbour authorities under local legislation that may be used to regulate harbour areas:

Byelaws – power to issue byelaws, subject to confirmation by the Secretary of State for Transport. Byelaws may apply to harbour land as well as the water

Special directions – power to issue directions in relation to individual ships in the harbour area for a specified purpose

General directions – power to issue directions in relation to all ships in the harbour area either in response to a particular occurrence or as a standing instruction to all ships or specified Classes of ship

Pilotage directions – (applies to 'competent harbour authorities' only) power to direct that it is compulsory for a ship to be subject to pilotage, i.e. under the charge of either an authorised pilot or an officer holding a Pilotage Exemption Certificate (PEC).

An industry-led National Directions Panel (NDP) provides guidance on the operational use of harbour directions. It also issues draft model directions as guides for harbour authorities and keeps under review the non-statutory Code of Conduct on the use of harbour directions.

8.3   Pilotage

8.3.1   Responsibility for pilotage

Pilotage is the navigation and control of a ship in confined waters, particularly on entering harbours, when responsibility is discharged by the Master to a local mariner expert. Pilotage was deregulated in the 1980s when the responsibility for providing all aspects of pilotage was transferred to harbour authorities.

Figure 8.2: Pilots provide professional guidance on local waters and are often mandatory for large vessels

Competent harbour authorities have specific powers under the Pilotage Act 1987 to enable them to discharge the pilotage duties imposed under that Act. The Act requires them to consider the need for pilotage to ensure the safety of vessels navigating within harbour areas, taking account of the size and nature of the harbour itself, the volume and size of traffic using the harbour, and the interests of other users.

Particular pilotage arrangements address the hazards involved in the carriage of dangerous goods or harmful substances by ship and each competent harbour authority provides the pilotage services that it considers necessary.

When a competent harbour authority decides, in the interests of safety, that pilotage should be compulsory in the harbour or any part of it, then the authority must issue pilotage directions. The directions must specify how and to which vessels they apply.

An authority will consult first with the owners of ships using the area where directions would apply and then with any other person carrying on marine operations within the harbour. HM ships are not subject to pilotage directions. In some ports, local legislation provides for licensed watermen and related categories and the pilotage directions may then exclude the vessels on which they work.

An authority is not necessarily obliged to issue directions covering all the circumstances for which it is considered that a pilotage service should be provided. There may be other circumstances in which it remains appropriate for the Master of a vessel, rather than the authority, to decide whether or not a pilot should be taken. The Master of a vessel not subject to pilotage directions has a right to request a pilot and the authority must decide whether it is obliged to provide such a service, paying particular attention to potential safety concerns.

Each competent harbour authority may authorise suitably qualified pilots in its area. Authorisations may relate to ships of a particular description and to particular parts of the harbour. The authority determines the qualifications for authorisation in respect of age, medical fitness standards, time of service, local knowledge, skill and character. It may also, after giving notice and allowing a reasonable opportunity to make representations, suspend or revoke an authorisation if it appears to the authority that the authorised person is guilty of any incompetence or misconduct affecting his capability as a pilot, or has ceased to have, or failed to provide evidence of, the required qualifications.

Courtesy of Danny Cornelissen

Figure 8.3: A pilot joining a vessel via a pilot ladder

The provision of pilotage services is one of the most important responsibilities of any harbour authority and in many ports it requires experienced, qualified mariners to provide safe and reliable pilotage services. Safety is of paramount concern not only for the ship entering the harbour but for the pilots who are required to both embark and disembark ships in all weathers, often at a considerable distance from shore. Pilot launches, and in some locations helicopters, are used to effect these transfers.

8.3.2 Pilotage exemption certificates

The Marine Navigation Act 2013 includes three sections that further simplify pilotage and amends the Pilotage Act 1987 in relation to the granting, use, suspension and withdrawal of Pilotage Exemption Certificates (PECs). It:

- Requires the Master of a ship who intends to use a Pilotage Exemption Certificate to specify the Certificate holder who will pilot the ship to the Competent Harbour Authority

- Extends the circumstances in which a Pilotage Exemption Certificate may be suspended or revoked

- Enables any deck officer of a ship, who meets the requirements for skill, experience, local knowledge and standard of English, to be awarded a Pilotage Exemption Certificate.

8.4 Protection Against Unreasonable Charges

The Harbours Act 1964 enables harbour authorities to impose ship, passenger and goods dues (harbour dues) and defines how they are applied to ships, passengers, goods and port services. Harbour authorities have the power to charge ship, passenger and goods dues as they think fit, although certain charges levied by harbour authorities are legally subject to the charges being 'reasonable'. A procedure exists for objections to be made in cases where charges are thought to be unreasonable, although appeals are rare.

8.5 The General Lighthouse Authorities (GLAs)

The Merchant Shipping Acts give the GLAs statutory duty for superintendence and management of all aids to navigation, i.e. all lighthouses, buoys and electronic aids in their area, and makes the Secretary of State for Transport statutorily responsible for the administration of the General Lighthouse Fund. The GLF is, therefore, a public fund managed by DfT into which the light dues levied on ships and all other GLA income is paid. The costs of providing UK aids to navigation are met from this fund of light dues receipts and so light dues exist as a levy, charge or tax on UK and foreign shipowners using UK ports.

The Light Dues rate is revised annually. In 2017/18, the charge is 37.5p per Net Registered Tonne (NRT), chargeable up to a Tonnage Cap of 40,000 NRT. The charge for large vessels, subject to certain exemptions, is therefore a not inconsiderable £15,000 per port call. However, vessels are subject to a maximum of 9 charges per year, so the maximum fee for a single vessel would be £135,000.

Figure 8.4: Perch Rock Lighthouse

The provision of aids to navigation in the waters of the UK and Eire is performed by three separate GLAs:

- Trinity House, for the waters of England

- The Commissioners of Northern Lighthouses, known as the Northern Lighthouse Board, for Scotland and the Isle of Man

- The Commissioners of Irish Lights, for Irish waters including those of Northern Ireland.

The mission of the GLAs is to deliver a reliable, efficient and cost-effective aid to navigation service for the benefit and safety of all mariners.

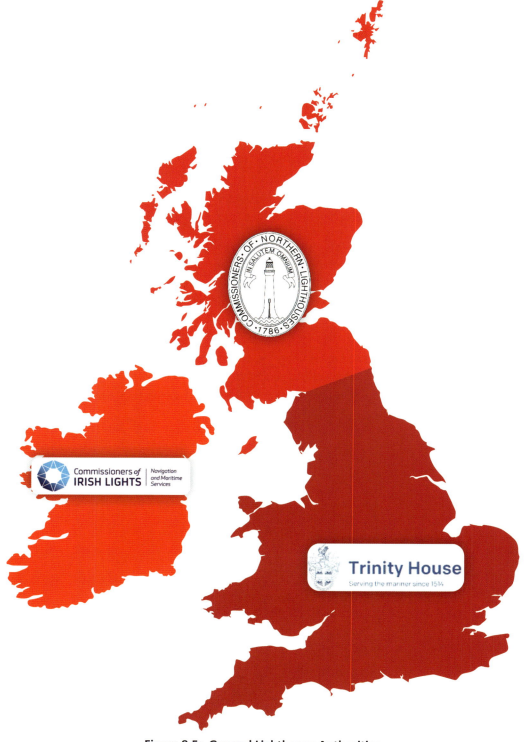

Figure 8.5: General Lighthouse Authorities

Key Point Summary

1) UK ports are vital to the economy and nationally we are well served by a mixture of ports under different ownership models.

2) Safe and efficient harbour operations for ships are managed by the Port Marine Safety Code (PMSC) and the granting of harbour directions.

3) Harbour authorities are responsible for pilotage, which is provided by local or contracted pilots and the issuance of Pilotage Exemption Certificates (PECs) to suitable mariners.

4) Harbour users are protected against unreasonable charges, although few appeals are made.

5) Aids to navigation in UK and Irish waters are provided by the three GLAs funded by means of light dues.

Customs Rules

9.1   Customs Controls and Maritime Trade

The primary purpose of customs controls is to regulate trade and to ensure that money due on goods entering the country is paid. Other functions have been grafted on to this core role, such as keeping prohibited items (such as drugs, weapons and counterfeit goods) out of the country and, more recently, screening items for security purposes. Fundamentally, however, customs procedures and customs law are designed to ensure the collection of Government revenue.

Customs controls are focused on the movement of goods, to ensure that the entry and departure of goods is recorded, that duty (taxation on the import or export of goods) is paid on them and that customs officers have suitable opportunities to stop goods and examine them to check that they are accurately and fully declared. The task of complying with customs controls primarily falls on the merchants who are buying and selling goods internationally (importers and exporters).

Figure 9.1: Border Force enforces trade regulations in UK waters

9.2   Obligations on Shipping Companies as Carriers of Goods

9.2.1   Scope of customs controls on the movement of goods by sea

Customs controls on goods entering or leaving the UK, and on the ships carrying those goods, differ depending on whether the goods are being moved within the EU or between the UK and a country outside the EU. Goods entering or leaving the EU are subject to customs control and all ships carrying them are accordingly subject to the requirements of customs law.

Moving goods within the EU is less clear-cut. Whether goods moving within the EU are subject to customs control or not depends on the customs 'status' of the goods themselves (i.e. whether they are EU goods or not). Ships on intra-EU voyages may be subject to customs requirements, depending on the voyage.

The movement of goods within the UK, whether by road or rail or coastal shipping, is not subject to customs control at all.

9.2.2   Ships arriving in the UK from outside the EU

Ships arriving at a UK port from outside the EU, and the cargo they are carrying, are subject to customs control. They are required to arrive at ports that have been approved by customs for handling international traffic, so as to ensure that appropriate facilities for customs control are in place, such as connections to customs inventory systems and (in some cases) examination sheds.

Ships are required to report their arrival, in advance, identifying themselves, where they have sailed from, itemising the cargo they are carrying and listing their crew and passengers (if any). This is known as pre-arrival notification.

Figure 9.2: Southampton, one of Britain's busiest ports

Historically, ships were also required to report their residual stocks of duty-free stores (such as alcohol and tobacco in the crew bond or held as stock for the ship's bars, restaurants and shops) and any dutiable or particularly valuable possessions belonging to the crew. These reporting requirements have changed and ships now have only to keep an onboard inventory of their duty-free stores and an onboard list of crews' effects, signed by the crew.

Customs interest is focused on the cargo. The ship's advance report of its cargo forms the first stage of a sequence of controls that continues until the cargo is either 'released to free circulation' (i.e. imported, with all duties and other taxes being paid on it) or taken out of the EU again. The sequence of controls on goods arriving from outside the EU is laid down in European law; the European Union is a Customs Union, comprising a single customs territory, throughout which a single body of EU rules applies. The arrival of goods at a UK port is, therefore, subject to the same requirements and procedures as would apply if the goods were arriving at a port in any other EU Member State. The same documentation must be submitted and the same duty must be paid.

Cargo reports, termed 'summary declarations', are required to be submitted electronically according to timescales that differ depending on the nature of the cargo and length of the voyage. In respect of containerised cargo, they are required to be submitted 24 hours before the ship starts loading in the overseas port (a requirement modelled on US security procedures and intended to enable Customs to prohibit the loading of cargo that is deemed to pose a security threat). In respect of bulk cargo, they are required four hours prior to the arrival of the ship in the UK port. A shorter timescale, of two hours prior to arrival, applies in the case of short sea voyages.

Shipping companies' customs obligations as carriers of goods cease once they have submitted these reports and landed the goods at an approved port (unless the goods are to be trans-shipped and taken out of the EU again). Subsequent stages of the customs process, such as importing the goods, warehousing or processing them, are the responsibility of other parties in the logistics chain. A shipping company can undertake some of these subsequent functions on behalf of the importer or other party, but is then acting as their agent rather than as carrier of the goods.

Figure 9.3: The Port of Dover, Britain's busiest ferry port

The most common circumstance in which a shipping company undertakes subsequent Customs functions is when importation is deferred until the goods reach their final destination. For the interim period, they are placed under 'transit', whereby a transit declaration is made at the port and guarantee is posted to cover the import duty, both of which are then discharged when the goods are subsequently imported. The decision about whether to defer importation in this way lies with the owner of the goods, as does the choice of which carrier will perform the onward movement, but such onwards movements are typically performed by the shipping company that brought the goods into the EU as part of a door-to-door service package.

9.2.3   Shipment of goods to a destination outside the EU

A similar process of customs controls applies to the departure of goods from the UK to a place outside the EU. Advance notice has to be given to Customs that the goods will be exported and the exporter of the goods is required to submit an export declaration. Once the export procedures have been completed, Customs will grant the shipping company permission to load the goods. Where no exporter exists, for example after goods have been trans-shipped at the port where they were landed, the obligation to declare the goods prior to departure falls to the shipping company.

Customs control on outbound goods legally comes to an end when the goods physically leave the EU. Few vessels sail directly from the UK to a port outside the EU and most UK exports are either trans-shipped in Continental ports or are carried on vessels that call at ports in other EU countries before sailing deep sea. Where such goods are loaded under a through Bill of Lading (B/L) (or equivalent document evidencing a single contract for their carriage from a place within the EU to a place outside it), Customs control ends at the first port of loading.

Ships are similarly required to report their departure to Customs. A stamped declaration, evidencing that the ship has been cleared outbound from the UK, may be demanded by the Customs authorities in the overseas port to which the ship is destined.

9.2.4   Sailings between the UK and other EU countries

Movements of goods within the EU are not subject to Customs control. European Customs authorities, alongside the police and other law enforcement agencies, are permitted to stop vehicles and check their contents where they have grounds for doing so, but routine controls on goods moving from one Member State to another are forbidden. Lorries and trains accordingly move freely across Europe, without having to report to, or being stopped by, Customs as they cross internal European frontiers between Member States.

Ships are treated differently. The Customs territory of the EU is defined as comprising the Member States and their territorial waters, which extend 12 nautical miles offshore. A ship that leaves territorial waters on a voyage between two Member States is regarded as having left the EU and, on arrival at its port of destination, is treated as having sailed from a port outside the EU. It is, therefore, required to report its arrival and its cargo to Customs. Its cargo is treated as originating from outside the EU and needs to be declared and duty paid. The EU status of cargo that originated in the EU can be re-established by an appropriate declaration on arrival at the destination port and the shipping company may (but is not obliged to) do this on behalf of the owner of the goods.

Ferries and other vessels (like feeder container ships) that operate scheduled services between EU ports only can, however, be approved by Customs as intra-EU services. Once approved, such 'regular shipping services' are treated as bridges between the ports at either end of the service. The ship operator is not required to report the arrival or departure of their ship to Customs and the cargo is not subject to Customs control on discharge. This means that lorries may drive straight off the ferry and out of the port without stopping (unless they are selected for an exceptional check) and that ferry operators are able to compete on an equal footing with the Channel Tunnel.

Passengers on such sailings are, similarly, not subject to Customs control, although they are liable to an immigration control. At some ports, the border control operates in a manner whereby the distinction between immigration control and customs control is not always obvious.

All international ferry routes to UK ports are approved as 'regular shipping services'. Vehicles and passengers arriving at a UK port by ferry may be stopped for a Customs examination only if there is individualised intelligence (relating to them) that they may be engaged in smuggling.

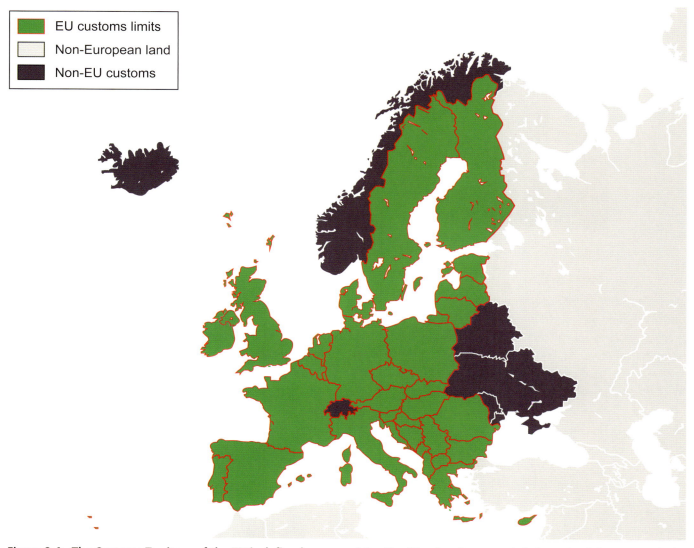

Figure 9.4: The Customs Territory of the EU is defined as comprising the Member States and their territorial waters, which extend 12 nautical miles offshore

9.3 Customs Control of Ships' Stores and Equipment

Items that are destined for use on board ships are treated differently in Customs law from those destined for use ashore. For the most part, this is a matter of excise duties and related procedures rather than customs duties. Excise duties are taxes on the domestic consumption of specific items, most obviously alcohol, tobacco and oil. (Customs duties, by contrast, are taxes on importation).

Alcohol and tobacco may be loaded onto ships' stores without the payment of excise duty. Approval from Customs is required on each occasion to ensure that the quantities loaded are reasonable and to provide a documentary record of the release of duty-free stock by the supplier. Once on board the ship, the items may similarly be released for consumption on board, either by being sold or given away, without triggering any liability for duty. To ensure that they are consumed on board, restrictions typically apply to the quantity that may be released at any one time, i.e. single packets of 20 cigarettes and alcohol in individual measures or in bottles that are opened on release.

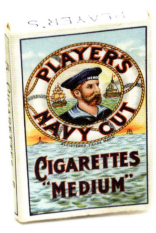

Figure 9.5: Alcohol and tobacco are liable to excise duty as well as customs duty

Rules relating to the sale from the ship's shop of alcohol and tobacco as merchandise for taking away by passengers differ depending on the nature of the ship's voyage. Items sold on domestic voyages attract the normal UK duty rate. Items sold on voyages between EU countries attract duty at the rate prevailing in the country in whose waters the sale takes place (in practice meaning that all sales take place in the waters of the country with the lower duty rate) and items sold on a voyage to or from a country outside the EU (or a cruise that includes a port in a country outside the EU) may be sold duty-free. In this last case, the passenger is responsible for declaring the items to Customs and paying the duty on disembarkation if carrying more than their usual duty-free allowance.

Ships may also load fuel and lubricating oil without payment of duty on the basis of a written application to Customs. Marine diesel may be marked with a red dye in order to prevent it being used in road vehicles, except where the fuel is supplied as bunkers or refined and shipped outside the UK for sale. Heavy fuel oil, which cannot be burned in normal engines, is also not dyed. Duty normally has to be paid on any duty-free oil re-landed from ships, but a special exemption exists for slops and other waste oil landed for proper disposal ashore.

Figure 9.6: The supply of bunker fuel is subject to customs regulations

Items imported to the UK for supply to seagoing ships as equipment are exempt from customs duty. As well as machinery and spare parts for the ship, eligible equipment includes items such as clothing, cutlery and furniture. Food and drink is excluded, as is tobacco.

Key Point Summary

1) Ships on international voyages are subject to Customs requirements as an extension of the Customs controls that apply to the cargo they are carrying.

2) In broad terms, the ship is permitted to land and load cargo only at ports that have been approved and is required to provide advance information about itself, its cargo, its crew and any passengers.

3) Ferries (and comparable liner services) sailing between EU ports only and which have been registered with Customs are treated as bridges on which the rules on free movement of goods within the Single Market apply in full, so that no customs formalities apply to the ship or to its cargo.

4) Ships' stores, fuel and equipment are exempt from duty; controls apply to the supplying of such items to ships so as to ensure that they are actually delivered to ships.

Passenger Shipping

10.1 Carriage of Passengers

Ferry operators and cruise lines are governed by the law of common carriage. They advertise their services to the public and are obliged to carry any passenger who pays the fare and fulfils the terms and conditions of carriage. This distinguishes them from owners or operators of passenger craft who offer their vessels for private charter, for example as a venue for a party.

Provided that a person has paid for a ticket and has satisfied the other terms and conditions of carriage, the sole circumstance in which the ferry or cruise operator may refuse to carry him is where his behaviour puts other passengers at risk or causes a nuisance, where the person is drunken and disorderly for example.

Ferry and cruise operators set their own terms and conditions of carriage. They are largely free to do so, subject to a general duty not to impose any that are unreasonable. Typical terms and conditions prohibit passengers from bringing hazardous articles on board the vessel, require them to comply with various security-related checks prior to embarkation and (on international voyages) to be in possession of the passports and visas they may require on disembarkation.

However, the carriage of passengers is more heavily regulated than the carriage of (most) cargoes. The regulatory framework is becoming ever more complex, as laws relating to consumer protection and non-discrimination are applied to ferry and cruise services and laws designed to control and tax individuals' behaviour ashore are applied to ships. International services are subject to the further burden of compliance with immigration law and tax rules are more complex when a ship passes through more than one tax jurisdiction.

10.2 Regulated Aspects of Passenger Carriage

10.2.1 Consumer protection

Travelling by ferry or cruise ship is, usually, an elective, recreational activity. Because of this, operators are driven by a strong commercial imperative to deliver excellent standards of service, because their business depends on persuading passengers to travel and, after they have done it once, persuading them to repeat the experience. A commitment to excellent service is, therefore, fundamental to their business and the quality of service provided to passengers is high.

Since the end of 2012, an EU regime of statutory passenger rights has prescribed how ferry and cruise operators must treat passengers whose sailings are delayed or cancelled. As soon as an operator knows that a sailing will be late, they are required to inform passengers who are waiting for it and to provide them with an updated sailing time as soon as possible. Where passengers are stuck in a port for more than 90 minutes waiting for a ship to sail, the operator is required to provide them with refreshments. Where they are stuck overnight, the operator is required to offer them accommodation. This is subject, in all cases, to such food, drink and accommodation being available at or near the port and to the operator having personnel on site to distribute it. Passengers whose sailings are cancelled or delayed by more than 90 minutes are entitled to cancel their bookings and cash in their tickets without penalty or to be rebooked on an alternative sailing.

Operators are also required to compensate passengers who arrive late at their destination, by reimbursing a percentage of their ticket price. The percentage reimbursement depends on a combination of the length of the voyage and how much later than advertised the ship reaches its destination. No such reimbursement is payable when the delay is due to bad weather or other factors beyond the operator's control, such as strikes, riots or the ship being diverted mid-voyage in order to assist in a search and rescue operation.

Figure 10.1: Passengers on board a ferry

These statutory prescriptions very largely reflect what operators already did to take care of their passengers as and when services were disrupted and the success of those long established arrangements is reflected in the low numbers of recorded complaints from passengers. The EU regime requires passengers' complaints to regulators to be recorded and in the first two years of the regime there were just 19 complaints about how passengers were treated when sailings were delayed or cancelled, in the context of more than 130 million passenger journeys.

The rights of passengers travelling by sea or inland waterway (for journeys of more than 500 m, using motorised vessels carrying more than 12 passengers and three crew members) can be enforced only if (1) the port of embarkation or (2) the port of destination is situated in the EU and if the service is operated by a European Union carrier. Cruise-ship passengers must embark at an EU port in order to enjoy these rights and are not covered by some of the provisions concerning delays.

Cancellation or delay of over 90 minutes on departure

- *passengers should be informed of the delay or cancellation no later than 30 minutes after the scheduled departure time;*

- *a choice between (i) being rerouted or continuing their journey as soon as possible, or (ii) being reimbursed within seven days (and, if necessary, a free return journey to the initial point of departure) should be offered;*

- *assistance (except if the passenger was informed of the delay before purchasing the ticket): meals, if possible, and accommodation on board or on land, if necessary. Accommodation on land is restricted to three nights at a cost of EUR 80 per night. Accommodation need not be provided if the cancellation or delay is caused by bad weather.*

Compensation should be paid within one month at the request of the passenger (except if he or she was informed of the delay before purchasing the ticket or if the delay was caused by bad weather or force majeure) as follows:

Compensation	25% of the ticket price paid	50% of the ticket price paid
Journey ≤ 4 hours	Delay ≥ 1 hour	Delay ≥ 2 hours
Journey 4 to 8 hours	Delay ≥ 2 hours	Delay ≥ 4 hours
Journey 8 to 24 hours	Delay ≥ 3 hours	Delay ≥ 6 hours
Journey ≥ 24 hours	Delay ≥ 6 hours	Delay ≥ 12 hours

[from European Parliament's *Fact Sheets on the European Union: Passenger Rights*]

Separately, under the Athens Convention, operators are required to carry insurance that enables them to pay compensation in the event of the death or injury of a passenger or in the event of loss or damage of luggage. In those events, compensation is, however, payable only when the incident was due to operator fault or negligence. Such insurance is typically provided as part of standard P&I cover.

10.2.2 Disabled access

Under the same EU regime of passenger rights, ferry and cruise operators are required to carry disabled passengers, unless doing so would pose a safety risk, and to provide (free of charge) assistance if required for embarking the ship, moving around it and disembarking at the end of the voyage. They are similarly obliged to carry a disabled passenger's wheelchair or other mobility equipment, a blind passenger's guide dog and a companion if the passenger is incapable of travelling on their own, all for no charge, except in the case of companions on cruise ships.

Figure 10.2: Disabled access on ships is governed by EU legislation

Ferry and cruise operators are not required to modify the structure or layout of their ships to make them accessible to disabled passengers if they are not already so, nor are they required to replace vessels that are not accessible. However, where an operator does order a new vessel, its design is expected to follow guidelines (originally laid down by the IMO in 1996) to ensure that it accommodates the needs of disabled passengers. This arrangement ensures that the fleet is becoming progressively more accessible over time without compromising the safety calculations underpinning the design of existing vessels.

Large numbers of disabled passengers and others with reduced mobility, such as the elderly, travel by ferry and cruise ships, and have done so for many years. Again, complaints are recorded on a national basis and just six complaints, all of which were resolved, were recorded in the two-year period of 2013 and 2014.

Ferry and cruise terminals, like other buildings in the UK where services are provided to the public, are required to be accessible to the disabled and to be modified if they are not.

10.2.3 Licensing and control of onboard activities

The application to passenger ships of licensing and social regulatory regimes that apply ashore varies according to the nature of the voyage. This reflects the legal constraints on regulating the internal economy of vessels in territorial waters and the practical difficulties of administering regimes on board to premises that move.

Figure 10.3: Passenger ships, including ferries, are licensed for alcohol sale and consumption

The ban on smoking in enclosed public spaces, for example, does not apply to ships in UK waters, nor to UK-flagged ships elsewhere. When the ban was introduced onshore in the UK, there had been a firm intention to apply it to ships as well, but a combination of legal objections and practical difficulties meant that this did not happen. The United Nations Convention on the Law of the Sea (UNCLOS) prevents the ban from being applied to non-UK-flagged vessels sailing within UK waters, including to or from a UK port. The practical challenge of enforcing a ban is obvious and, in the absence of statutory controls, ferry and cruise operators provide a smoke-free environment on board their vessels conforming to norms that their passengers expect.

Figure 10.4: Despite the absence of statutory controls, ferry and cruise operators provide a smoke-free environment on board their vessels

Licensing requirements related to the sale of alcohol and entertainment do apply to ferries and cruise ships, but only on domestic voyages within the UK. Ships on international voyages are outside the scope of the licensing regime. For ships on domestic voyages where alcohol is served or entertainment provided, a premises licence is required. Licences are issued by the local authority responsible for the area where the vessel is usually moored or berthed. The licensing procedure is simpler than for premises ashore because the local authority should rely on the certificates issued to the vessel by the Maritime and Coastguard Agency (MCA) to confirm that the public safety objectives of the licensing regime have been met. As with pubs and bars ashore, there is a separate requirement for the individual who is designated as responsible for the sale of alcohol on the ship to hold a personal licence.

Figure 10.5: An example of a passenger space on board a ferry

The separate regime for licensing casinos and other types of gambling (such as slot machines) on ships applies in an identical manner: ships on domestic voyages require a licence, which is issued by the local authority for the place where the vessel is usually moored or berthed, but ships whose voyages take them into international waters are outside the scope of the regime.

Contrary to popular perception, it is not possible to get married on a UK-flagged cruise vessel or ferry (unless the ship is berthed at a place in Scotland that has been registered for that purpose). Successive Shipping Ministers have suggested that the law could be changed to allow UK-flagged ships to host wedding ceremonies and for the Master of the ship to officiate them, in the same way as happens already on ships operating under a number of other Flags, but no such change has occurred.

Figure 10.6: Contrary to popular perception, it is not possible to get married on a UK-flagged cruise ship

Any births or deaths that occur on a UK-flagged ship must be recorded by the Master and then relayed to the MCA, for onward submission to the General Register Office.

10.3 Border Controls

Figure 10.7: UK Border Controls at Calais

Passengers arriving in the UK from other countries are subject to border controls. These vary depending on where the ship has sailed from, whether the ship is a ferry or a cruise ship and the infrastructure at the port of arrival. In most instances, the most significant element of the control is examination of the passenger's passport by an officer of the Border Force.

There are no ferry sailings to the UK from outside the European Union, but cruise ships arriving from outside the EU are subject to immigration and customs controls. Passengers arriving from elsewhere in the EU (except Ireland), whether on a cruise ship or by ferry, are subject to immigration control only, although they may exceptionally be stopped for a customs check as well. Those arriving from the Republic of Ireland, the Channel Islands, or the Isle of Man are not subject to any routine border controls but may exceptionally be stopped for a passport and/or a customs check. Passengers arriving from any destination may be stopped by the police for counter-terrorism purposes, or by health officials in the event of an epidemic.

Domestic voyages within the UK are not subject to any border controls, because they do not involve the crossing of any borders, but ferry services between Great Britain and Northern Ireland are monitored closely by the police, who sometimes refer to their activities as border policing.

At most UK ferry ports and at cruise terminals, UK border controls are carried out shortly after passengers have disembarked. On ferry services to Dover from Calais and Dunkirk, immigration control is performed in France prior to sailing, with only the exceptional customs and police stops being performed in Dover. French inbound passport controls, on sailings from Dover, are carried out before passengers leave the UK (a similar arrangement operates at the Channel Tunnel.) At ports where cruise vessels call but where there is no terminal building, border controls are either performed at the ship's door or by 'crossing officers' during the inbound voyage.

Individual passengers are responsible for stopping at the checkpoint and presenting their passports, and ferry and cruise operators are obliged to check that passengers are in possession of passports and, if necessary, visas prior to embarkation for a voyage to the UK (except at Calais and Dunkirk, where the Border Force itself has already checked the passenger). They are also liable for the cost of removing a person who is refused entry by the Border Force on arrival in the UK, where the person arrived on their ship. Hauliers are responsible for preventing people from hiding in their lorries and evading UK border controls.

Operators of cruise ships sailing between the UK and a place outside the EU are required to provide a manifest showing the passport data of all passengers (and crew). There is no requirement to provide such manifests on sailings between the UK and other countries in the EU, but cruise operators nonetheless do so and ferry operators share the manifest data that they have. Ferry and cruise operators also collect the passport data of passengers leaving the UK on routes that are subject to immigration control and share it with the Border Force.

10.4 Taxation of Onboard Sales

Sales to passengers on board vessels on domestic voyages within the UK are taxed as they would be if they took place ashore. Sales on international voyages are taxed differently, reflecting the fact that liability to tax (and the rate of it) varies according to where the sale takes place. Sales on voyages between the UK and a place outside the EU (including on cruises where the itinerary includes a port that is outside the EU) are generally treated as being outside the scope of UK tax.

Sales on intra-EU voyages are taxed according to a complex set of rules laid down by the EU, which are intended to reconcile the principle that all sales made within the EU should be taxed acknowledging the reality that sales taxes and excise duties differ from one EU country to another. For sales from the ship's shop, excise duty is charged at the rate applicable in the country in whose waters the sale occurs (which, in practice, means that all sales take place in the waters of the country with the lower duty rate), while VAT is charged at the rate applying in the country of departure. Sales from bars and restaurants on the ship are duty free and treated as outside the scope of VAT.

Figure 10.8: Onboard sales are subject to various tax regimes, depending on operational area

Revenue from casinos and slot machines on board ships on international voyages is treated as outside the scope of UK tax, provided it is not earned while the ship is in port. In practice, therefore, ships keep their casinos shut and slot machines switched off while in UK ports.

Key Point Summary

1) Ferry and cruise operators are required by law to compensate passengers who arrive late at their destination, except where the delay is not the operator's fault, and to take care of passengers stranded at terminals waiting for a sailing.

2) Ferry and cruise operators are required to carry disabled passengers where they can do so safely, but are not required to modify their vessels specially.

3) Social licensing regimes to regulate the sale of alcohol and gambling apply only on domestic voyages and legal difficulties prevent them applying to international voyages.

4) Passengers travelling from overseas are subject to border controls, which differ according to the nature of the voyage. Ferry and cruise operators are liable for some elements of the control.

5) Sales on domestic voyages are taxed as if they were made ashore, while those on international voyages are mostly outside the scope of UK tax unless they take place on voyages within the EU, in which case a complex set of EU rules applies.

Glossary

Able or Ordinary Seafarer – a rating in the deck and/or engine department of a ship who is qualified in accordance with either the ILO Certification of Able Seamen Convention, 1946 or the STCW Convention.

Admiralty law – maritime law. In the UK, most maritime law cases are tried in the Admiralty Division of the High Court of Justice.

Ballast – water used to improve the stability and control of the ship. Ballast water is located in multiple tanks across the length of the ship, which are flooded or emptied with seawater as necessary. Generally, a ship will discharge its ballast water as cargo is loaded on board and will take on ballast water again as cargo is unloaded.

Bareboat charter – an arrangement for the chartering or hiring of a ship or boat, whereby no crew or provisions are included as part of the agreement; the people who rent the vessel from the owner are responsible for provision of these items.

Bill of lading – a document used in international trade that has three specific roles:

1) Acts as a cargo receipt issued by a carrier detailing a shipment of merchandise

2) Acts as evidence of the contract of carriage (not the contract itself)

3) Gives title of that shipment to a specified party.

Bulk carrier – a type of ship carrying bulk cargoes in accordance with the IMSBC Code. This is usually a ship with large holds carrying such cargoes as grain, iron ore and coal.

Bunkers – fuel oil burned in a ship's main engines (auxiliaries typically use diesel). Bunkering is the process of transferring fuel from one vessel to another.

Cabotage – the domestic transport of goods or passengers by a transport operator from another country. Cabotage rights are the right of a company from one country to trade in another country.

Captain – see Master.

Category A–D waters:

- Category A: Narrow rivers and canals where the depth of water is generally less than 1.5 metres

- Category B: Wider rivers and canals where the depth of water is generally 1.5 metres or more and where the significant wave height is not expected to exceed 0.6 metres at any time

- Category C: Tidal rivers and estuaries and large, deep lakes and lochs where the significant wave height is not expected to exceed 1.2 metres at any time

- Category D: Tidal rivers and estuaries where the significant wave height is not expected to exceed 2.0 metres at any time.

Charterer – a person or company who hires a ship from a shipowner for a period of time (time charter) or who reserves the entire cargo space for a single voyage (voyage charter).

Chief Officer – the senior officer of the deck department, below the Master. Chief Officers will usually be responsible for the maintenance of the deck and are in charge of all cargo operations in port.

Class – a standard of construction for ships, usually derived from standards produced by the International Association of Classification Societies (IACS). Individual Classification Societies such as Lloyds Register will verify whether a ship is 'in Class' and therefore in compliance with the standards.

COLREGs – the International Regulations for Preventing Collisions at Sea, also known as the IRPCS. If correctly followed, they ensure that ships will avoid collision by altering course away from each other or by proceeding at a safe speed.

Container – a standard box of length 20 or 40 ft, width 8 ft and height 8 ft 6 in. High cube containers are 9 ft 6 in high. Containers are usually transported on dedicated container ships, which carry out a liner service between global ports. However, feeder ships may carry container cargoes between smaller distances and close ports. Generally, other ships may take containers as a type of deck cargo.

Deadweight tonnage (DWT) – a measure of the carrying capacity of a vessel, i.e. how much weight the ship is carrying or can safely carry. DWT is the sum of the weights of cargo, fuel, fresh water, ballast water, provisions, passengers and crew. NB: it does not include the weight of the ship.

Deck department – the department responsible for the safe navigation of the ship, as well as cargo operations and operational procedures. It consists of the bridge officers, including the Master and Chief Officer, as well as any deck ratings and the Bosun.

Demurrage – the financial penalty paid by a shipping company when a cargo is not transferred as requested or the vessel is not able to fulfil the requirements of the charter party agreement (see also Laytime).

Displacement – the weight of water that is displaced by the volume of the ship's hull (Archimedes principle).

Document of Compliance (DOC) – a document issued to a company when the shoreside aspects of the Safety Management System (SMS) are found to fully comply with the requirements of the ISM Code. The DOC is specific to the ship type.

Draught – the depth of the ship's keel below the waterline (this is where the hull of a ship meets the surface of the water). Safe draught requirements are contained within the Load Line Convention.

Drydock – a constructed basin or raised watertight unit, usually within a shipyard, that allows for maintenance, construction and repair of a ship. Water can be drained from the dock to allow access to the ship's hull, which would normally be below the waterline.

ECDIS – an electronic chart display and information system. This is an aid to navigation, containing charts in electronic form. It is connected to other onboard equipment such as the compass and GPS.

EEA – European Economic Area.

Engine department – the department responsible for the engine room and ship's machinery. It usually consists of the Chief Engineer, his officers and a small team of ratings who act as motormen, cleaners and greasers.

Flag State – where the ship is registered, i.e. its port of registry and the nation that port is in. For example, a ship registered in London, will be flagged within the United Kingdom.

Freeboard – the vertical distance between the waterline and the top of the hull, measured at the lowest point where water can enter the boat or ship.

Freight rates – financial charges made by a shipping company for the transport of cargo on its ships from one destination to another.

Gross tonnage – a calculated unitless index related to a ship's overall internal volume.

IMO – the International Maritime Organization is the global body responsible for shipping and is a constituent part of the United Nations. Through senior committees such as MSC (Maritime Safety Committee) and MEPC (Maritime Environmental Protection Committee), nations agree on codes and conventions that apply to shipping and are enforced by Member States.

IOPC Funds – the International Oil Pollution Compensation Funds are two intergovernmental organisations (the 1992 Fund and the Supplementary Fund) that provide compensation for oil pollution damage resulting from spills of persistent oil from tankers. They are funded by a levy paid by ports and terminals that receive over 150,000 tonnes of oil in a year.

ISM Code – the International Safety Management (ISM) Code is the primary code for the safe management of ships. There are provisions that apply to companies and ships. A company will receive a DOC if found to be compliant with the Code.

ISPS Code – the International Ship and Port Facility Security (ISPS) Code is an amendment to the Safety of Life at Sea (SOLAS) Convention on minimum security arrangements for ships, ports and government agencies.

Laytime – usually measured in lay days, this refers to the time in days when a ship is not in service due to bad weather, machinery failure or other unexpected delays.

MARPOL – the International Convention for the Prevention of Pollution from Ships. MARPOL ensures that minimum standards are in place to prevent pollution from oil, chemicals, garbage, sewage and other pollutants.

Master – the captain of a merchant ship, who has command of the ship and is responsible for the safety of all persons and property on board, and for ensuring successful completion of each voyage.

MCA – the Maritime and Coastguard Agency is a specialised agency of the UK government responsible for shipping and seafarers.

Merchant Navy – the broad term for those who serve on ships at sea, extending generally to private commerce and merchant going ships.

MLC – the Maritime Labour Convention details the minimum international requirements for the welfare of ships' crews. It covers topics such as insurance, rest hours, accommodation design and leave pay.

MODU – Mobile Offshore Drilling Units are facilities designed or modified to engage in drilling and exploration activities. They include drilling vessels, semi-submersibles, submersibles, jack-ups, and similar facilities that can be moved without substantial effort.

Mooring – this is the process of tying up a vessel with ropes or wires to stop its movement. Usually, mooring takes place alongside a berth in a port, but it may also take place next to a fixed sea buoy.

Net Tonnage (NT) – a dimensionless index calculated from the total moulded volume of the ship's cargo spaces by using a mathematical formula, as defined in the International Convention on Tonnage Measurement of Ships that was adopted by the IMO in 1969.

Officers – licensed mariners who have undertaken training in accordance with STCW and passed an oral exam to be awarded a certificate of competency. They include Deck Officers and Engineering Officers.

Operating costs (OPEX) – expenses involved in the day-to-day running of a ship and incurred whatever trade the ship is engaged in. They include crew wages and expenses, victualing, stores, spares, repairs and maintenance, lubricants and insurance.

Paris/Tokyo MoUs – these Port State Control regimes consist of a number of participating maritime Administrations and aim to eliminate the operation of sub-standard ships through a harmonised system of Port State Control.

Pilot – an individual with a specific knowledge of local waters or certain ship types. A pilot will board a ship either from ashore, if the ship is departing in port, or from the sea via a pilot boat and pilot ladder. In the UK, pilots are mandatory within certain harbour authorities, although ships' officers are, in certain cases, able to obtain Pilotage Exemption Certificates.

P&I Club – protection and indemnity insurance, more commonly known as 'P&I' insurance, is a form of mutual maritime insurance provided by a P&I Club. Whereas a marine insurance company provides 'hull and machinery' cover for shipowners and cargo cover for cargo owners, a P&I Club provides cover for open-ended risks that traditional insurers are reluctant to insure. Typical P&I cover includes a carrier's third-party risks for damage caused to cargo during carriage, war risks and risks of environmental damage, such as oil spills and pollution.

Port State Control (PSC) – the inspection of foreign ships in other national ports by PSC officers (inspectors) for the purpose of verifying that the competency of the Master and officers on board and the condition of the ship and its equipment comply with the requirements of international conventions and that the vessel is manned and operated in compliance with international law. Port State Control regimes such as the Paris MoU ensure that efforts are coordinated between Flag States.

Reefer – a container used to transport refrigerated or frozen cargo.

RoRo – Roll-on/Roll-off ships carry wheeled cargo (such as cars and trucks) that is driven on and off the ship on its own wheels or using a platform vehicle, such as a self-propelled modular transporter. This is in contrast to lift-on/lift-off (LoLo) vessels, which use a crane to load and unload cargo.

Safe Manning Document – a document issued by a ship's Flag State that must be carried by all ships of 500 GT or above. It indicates the minimum requirements (in respect of numbers, qualifications and experience) of personnel serving on board. Beginning a voyage without complying with the Safe Manning Document is an offence.

Shipyard – an industrial facility where ships are constructed, repaired and maintained. Also known as a dockyard. Shipyards commonly include one or more drydocks.

Short Sea Shipping – shipping that mainly operates along a coast, without crossing an ocean. Conversely, deep sea shipping is trans-oceanic.

SOLAS – the International Convention for the Safety of Life at Sea, concerned with the safe building and operation of ships.

STCW – the International Convention on Standards of Training, Certification and Watchkeeping for Seafarers. This sets qualification standards for personnel working on seagoing merchant ships. It was adopted in 1978 and significantly amended in 1995.

Tanker – a ship that is primarily designed to carry liquid cargoes in bulk. Such cargoes may include oil, chemicals and LNG.

Territorial waters – as defined by the 1982 United Nations Convention on the Law of the Sea (UNCLOS), a belt of coastal waters extending at most 12 nautical miles from the baseline (usually the mean low-water mark) of a coastal State. The territorial sea is regarded as the sovereign territory of the State, although foreign ships are permitted innocent passage through it.

Time charter – where a ship is chartered for a specific time period. The owner still manages the vessel, but the charterer directs the ships to the required ports for the voyage(s).

Tramp ship – a ship that does not have a fixed schedule or published ports of call. The ideal tramp can carry anything to anywhere, and freight rates are influenced by supply and demand.

Voyage charter – where a ship is chartered for a specified number of trips/voyages.

Voyage costs – the cost of fuel, port expenses and canal costs specific to a voyage.

Further Reading

Organisations and Associations

British Ports Association

Commissioners of Irish Lights

EC Directorate-General for Maritime Affairs and Fisheries (DG MARE)

EC Directorate-General for Mobility and Transport (DG MOVE)

European Maritime Safety Agency (EMSA)

General Lighthouse Authorities (GLAs)

International Association of Classification Societies (IACS)

International Hydrographic Organization (IHO)

International Labour Organization (ILO)

International Maritime Organization (IMO)

Marine Management Organisation (MMO)

Maritime and Coastguard Agency (MCA)

Northern Lighthouse Board

Trinity House

UK Hydrographic Office (UKHO)

UK Major Ports Group

Conventions, Resolutions and General Guidance

European Commission. *EU External Action Common Foreign and Security Policy – Sanctions Policy.*

European Commission. *Liability of carriers of passengers by sea in the event of accidents – Regulation (EC) No 392/2009.*

European Commission. *System of Mandatory Surveys for the Safe Operation of Regular Ro-Ro and High-Speed Passenger Craft Services – EU Council Directive 1999/35.*

European Commission. *The EU Guidelines on State Aid to Maritime Transport.*

European Commission. *The EU Package Travel Directive – Directive (EU) 2015/2302.*

European Commission. *The EU Passenger Rights Regime – Regulation (EU) No 1177/2010.*

European Commission. *The EU Cabotage Regime – Council Regulation (EEC) No 3577/92.*

European Commission. *The principle of freedom to provide services to maritime transport between Member States and between Member States and third countries – Council Regulation (EEC) No 4055/86.*

European Commission. *The Union Customs Code – Regulation (EU) No 952/2013.*

HMRC. *The Tonnage Tax Manual.*

HMRC. *UK Government Guidance on Seafarers' Earnings Deduction.*

ILO. *The Maritime Labour Convention, 2006.*

IMO. *Athens Convention relating to the Carriage of Passengers and their Luggage by Sea (PAL).*

IMO. *International Convention for the Prevention of Pollution from Ships, 1973*, as modified by the Protocol of 1978 relating thereto and by the Protocol of 1997 (MARPOL).

IMO. *International Convention for the Safety of Life at Sea (SOLAS), 1974,* as amended.

IMO. *International Convention on Standards of Training, Certification and Watchkeeping for Seafarers, 1978* (STCW), as amended, including the 1995 and 2010 Manila Amendments.

IMO. *International Safety Management Code* (ISM Code), 2014.

IMO. *International Ship and Port Facility Security Code* (ISPS Code).

MCA. *Ship Security Guidance.*

MCA. *The Merchant Shipping Act 1995.*

MCA. *UK Classification and Certification Guidance.*

MCA. *UK Liability Insurance Requirements.*

MCA. *UK Ship Registration Guidance.*

OECD Council. *Recommendation of the OECD Council concerning Common Principles of Shipping Policy for Member countries – February 1987.*

The UK Chamber of Shipping. *The Bribery Act 2010: Practical Guidance for the UK Shipping Industry*, 2015.

UK Department for Transport. *UK Department for Transport interpretative guidance on EU Passenger Rights regime, 2010.*

UK Government. *Bribery Act 2010: Guidance to help commercial organisations prevent bribery.*

UK Government. *Carriage of Goods by Sea Act 1971.*

UK Government. *Carriage of Goods by Sea Act 1992.*

UK Government. *The Companies Act 2006.*

UK Government. *The Open Port Duty – Harbours, Docks and Piers Clauses Act 1847.*

UK Government. *Customs and Excise Management Act (CEMA) 1979.*

UK Government. *Port Marine Safety Code* (November 2016).

UK Government. *Marine Navigation Act 2013.*

UK Government. *Pilotage Act 1987.*

UK Home Office. *Guidance to Immigration Officers – Seamen – July 2014.*

Annex 1

Requirements of Certification

The certificates that must be carried for UK-registered vessels vary according to their type, gross tonnage, type of cargo and whether they are on a domestic or international voyage. Some ships may utilise the Alternative Compliance Scheme (ACS) in order to streamline the statutory certification process. Survey procedures and dates for all major ship certificates are harmonised according to the Harmonized System of Survey and Certification (HSSC) developed by the IMO.

The following is an outline of the main certification requirements.

- **Air pollution certificate** – for fishing vessels, passenger ships, cargo ships, oil tankers, chemical tankers or gas carriers and large commercial yachts of 400 GT or more. This certificate ensures compliance with MARPOL Annex VI.

- **Anti-fouling certificate** – for fishing vessels, passenger ships, cargo ships, oil tankers, chemical tankers or gas carriers and large commercial yachts of 400 GT or more. This certificate is issued in support of the International Convention on the Control of Harmful Anti-Fouling Systems on Ships which seeks to ensure only approved anti-fouling chemicals are used in order to minimise environmental damage through leeching.

- **Cargo ship safety certificate** – for cargo ships, oil tankers, chemical tankers or gas carriers and large commercial yachts over 300 GT. A certificate may be issued after survey to a cargo ship that complies with the relevant requirements of Chapters II-1, II-2, III, IV and V and other relevant requirements of SOLAS 1974 as modified by the 1988 SOLAS Protocol, as an alternative to the Cargo Ship Safety Construction Certificate, Cargo Ship Safety Equipment Certificate and Cargo Ship Safety Radio Certificate. A Record of Equipment for the Cargo Ship Safety Certificate (Form C) shall be permanently attached.

- **Cargo ship safety construction certificate** – for cargo ships, oil tankers, chemical tankers or gas carriers and large commercial yachts over 500 GT on international voyages only. A certificate shall be issued after survey to vessels that satisfy the requirements for cargo ships on survey, set out in regulation I/10 of SOLAS 1974, and comply with the applicable requirements of Chapters II-1 and II-2, other than those relating to fire-extinguishing appliances and fire-control plans.

- **Cargo ship safety equipment certificate** – for cargo ships, oil tankers, chemical tankers or gas carriers and large commercial yachts over 500 GT on international voyages only. A certificate shall be issued after survey to a cargo ship that complies with the relevant requirements of Chapters II-1 and II-2, III and V and any other relevant requirements of SOLAS 1974. A Record of Equipment for the Cargo Ship Safety Equipment Certificate (Form E) shall be permanently attached.

- **Cargo ship safety radio certificate** – for cargo ships, oil tankers, chemical tankers or gas carriers and large commercial yachts over 300 GT on international voyages only. The requirements are in accordance with SOLAS Chapter 4 and include the inspection of all radio equipment associated with life-saving appliances, adequacy of power supplies and the requisite number of personnel on board that are qualified to operate the equipment.

- **Certificate of fitness (chemical or gas) certificate** – for all chemical tankers or gas carriers. The award of this certificate ensures that the structure, equipment, systems, fittings, arrangements and materials must be surveyed to ensure compliance with the requirements of the following codes:

  » Code for the Construction and Equipment of Ships Carrying Dangerous Chemicals in Bulk (the BCH Code), for ships built prior to July 1986

  » International Code for the Construction and Equipment of Ships Carrying Dangerous Chemicals in Bulk (the IBC Code), for ships built after July 1986.

- **Dangerous goods certificate** – for passenger ships built after 1st September 1984 and for cargo ships after a certain date of build on international voyages only. Any of these vessels that carry dangerous goods must hold a certificate of compliance to ensure correct and safe handling and stowage. Dangerous goods are those that are listed within the International Maritime Dangerous Goods (IMDG) Code.

- **Load line certificate** – for passenger ships in non-UK waters, cargo ships, oil tankers, chemical tankers or gas carriers and large commercial yachts over 24 metres in length (if built on or after 21st July 1968) or of more than 150 GT and for passenger ships in UK waters over 80 net tonnes. In accordance with the International Convention on Load Lines (CLL 66/88), all assigned load lines must be marked amidships on each side of ships engaged in international voyages. The determinations of the freeboard of ships are calculated and verified by Classification Societies, which issue International Load Line Certificates.

- **Maritime Labour Convention certificate** – for ships of over 500 GT. It certifies that ships are in compliance with the requirements of the Maritime Labour Convention, which covers the working and living conditions of seafarers on board. Certificates are valid for five years, subject to an intermediate inspection by the competent authority.

- **Minimum safe manning document certificate** – for passenger ships, cargo ships, oil tankers, chemical tankers or gas carriers and large commercial yachts over 500 GT. It ensures that ships are manned with personnel of appropriate grades who have been properly trained and certificated. Specific requirements for safe manning are laid down in Regulation 14 of Chapter V SOLAS in order to ensure navigational safety. The numbers of certificated officers and certificated and non-certificated ratings must be sufficient to ensure safe and efficient operation of the ship at all times.

- **Oil pollution prevention certificate** – for fishing vessels, passenger ships, cargo ships, chemical tankers or gas carriers and large commercial yachts over 400 GT and oil tankers over 150 GT. The regulations aim to prevent oil in ships from being discharged into rivers or the sea. They include such requirements as an oil record book, oily water separating equipment, slop tanks, segregated water ballast tanks, crude oil washing arrangements (if applicable), limitation of size and protected location of segregated ballast tanks and cargo oil tanks, together with subdivision and stability criteria. Surveys include an examination of the structure, equipment, systems, fittings, arrangements, plans and material to ensure compliance with the requirements of the regulations.

- **Passenger ship safety certificate** – required for all passenger ships that carry more than 12 passengers. It requires an annual survey and covers the SOLAS requirements of ship stability and construction, the state of the hull, machinery, fire-fighting equipment, life-saving appliances and navigation and radio equipment.

- **Safety management certificate** – for all passenger ships and for cargo ships, oil tankers, chemical tankers or gas carriers and large commercial yachts over 500 GT. The award of this certificate confirms that an up-to-date Safety Management System is in place and is in accordance with the requirements of the ISM Code.

- **Sewage pollution certificate** – for fishing vessels, passenger ships, cargo ships, oil tankers, chemical tankers or gas carriers and large commercial yachts of 400 GT or more, or carrying 15 persons or more on international voyages only. The award of this certificate confirms that the ship has sewage treatment, handling and storage facilities on board that meet the requirements of MARPOL Annex IV.

- **Ship sanitation certificate** – for any ship on an international voyage. It requires a ship's compliance with the maritime sanitation and quarantine rules outlined in Article 39 of the International Health Regulations. A certificate is issued on arrival at port and is valid for six months.

- **Ship security certificate** – for passenger ships, cargo ships, oil tankers, chemical tankers or gas carriers and large commercial yachts on international voyages only. The award of this certificate confirms that the ship is complying fully with the International Ship and Port Facility Security (ISPS) Code and that an approved Ship's Security Plan is in place.